Emerging Perspectives on Assessment of Exceptional Children

Randy Elliot Bennett and Charles A. Maher
Editors

The Haworth Press
New York • London

Emerging Perspectives on Assessment of Exceptional Children has also been published as
Special Services in the Schools, Volume 2, Numbers 2/3, Winter 1985-86/Spring 1986.

The Haworth Press, Inc., 28 East 22 Street, New York, NY 10010-6194
EUROSPAN/Haworth, 3 Henrietta Street, London WC2E 8LU England

Library of Congress Cataloging-in-Publication Data
Emerging perspectives on assessment of exceptional
    children.

    Published also as v. 2, nos. 2/3, winter 1985-86/spring 1986 of Special services in the
schools.
    Includes bibliographies.
        1. Handicapped children—United States—Testing. 2. Handicapped children—
United States—Psychological testing. 3. Ability—Testing. I. Bennett, Randy Elliot,
1952-   . II. Maher, Charles A., 1944-
LC4031.E56   1986   371.9   86-3128
ISBN 0-86656-410-1

Emerging Perspectives on Assessment of Exceptional Children

Special Services in the Schools
Volume 2, Numbers 2/3

CONTENTS

Emerging Perspectives
on Assessment
of Exceptional Children

Emerging Perspectives on Assessment of Exceptional Children

Emerging Perspectives on Assessment of Exceptional Children: An Overview

Randy Elliot Bennett
Educational Testing Service

Charles A. Maher
Rutgers University

Assessment is the process of gathering and interpreting information about individual students for educational decision making (Maher & Bennett, 1984). The decisions based on assessment information typically include whether special education should be provided, what instructional goals should be specified, and in what placement setting activities to achieve those goals should be delivered. The importance of these decisions to the lives of individual students makes it critical that the assessment process produce trustworthy results.

Federal attempts to structure the assessment process so as to encourage the production of high quality information are only a decade or so old. Since these initial attempts at quality control, embodied in the rules and regulations for PL 93-380 and then PL 94-142, most school districts have made serious attempts to describe student functioning as accurately as possible. As any reading of the research literature that has evolved over this period will show, these attempts have not been fully successful. They have, in large part, been hampered by a dearth of quality assessment tools, staff that are not always well-trained, and an evaluation process that is subject to a variety of biasing influences and which produces little instructionally-relevant data (Bennett, 1983; Ysseldyke, 1983). Many school districts tried to address these problems but were often frustrated by

Requests for reprints should be sent to: Randy Elliot Bennett, Educational Testing Service, Princeton, NJ 08541.

1

a field that could not offer sound solutions grounded in a firm theoretical and empirical base.

The problems that hamper the accurate assessment of children still exist. The field is, however, beginning to offer alternatives that at least have the promise of being theoretically and empirically sound. Two major reasons can be offered for this growth. The more obvious reason is the effect of time. The problems affecting the quality of assessment information and the decisions based on that information are complex; sensible approaches to the solution of those problems required time to formulate and test.

The second, and perhaps more important reason for the appearance of promising approaches, is the integration of special education with other fields that has largely occurred over the past decade. Special education has always overlapped with such fields as speech therapy, school psychology, and rehabilitation. Now, more than ever, we are seeing a substantial integration of special education and its traditionally related fields with such nontraditional partners as cognitive and developmental psychology, neuroscience, computer science, engineering, and educational and psychological measurement. The partnerships that have resulted have taken the form of special educators doing work in these fields, of researchers from these fields applying their knowledge to special education, and of training programs that integrate these various areas of study.

This volume presents emerging perspectives on various topics related to the assessment of exceptional children and youth. For the most part, the perspectives presented reflect results of the partnership between special education and other fields.

The papers presented in the volume fall into four logical groups. The first set deals with assessment as a process. The four papers in this set integrate contributions from special education, school psychology, educational and psychological measurement, and computer science, among other areas. The first two papers, by Deno, Marston, and Tindall, and Bergan, present new approaches to the assessment process. The approaches delineated are particularly noteworthy for their emphasis on providing instructionally-useful information as a result of student assessment. The paper by Hasselbring describes a computerized consulting aid that may soon help manage assessment. Finally, Reschly provides commentary on improving the various aspects of the process.

The second group of papers focuses on the assessment of learner characteristics and borrows from work in cognitive and personality psychology, and from neuroscience. Spear and Sternberg, Feuerstein et al.; and Hartlage present different approaches to the measurement of cognitive functioning, with Spear and Sternberg, and Feuerstein discussing the topic from an information processing perspective, and Hartlage from a neuropsychological one. It is again worthy to note the emphasis on gathering information with clear instructional implications. The set is concluded with a paper on personality measurement by Barnett.

The third group of papers explores the assessment of three special populations. Lidz discusses evaluating the preschool child, noting the particular contributions of developmental psychology to this endeavor. Reynolds summarizes the report of his Federal task force on the technical problems tied to identifying students with learning disabilities (LD), and proposes an approach to LD diagnosis derived from educational and psychological measurement. Finally, Grise explores issues in certifying the skills of handicapped students impacted by minimum competency testing requirements.

The volume is concluded with a commentary by Yoshida and Friedman on the implications for special education of the latest revision of the *Standards for Educational and Psychological Testing* (American Psychological Association, 1985), sponsored by the American Educational Research Association, the American Psychological Association, and the National Council on Measurement in Education. The *Standards* brings together in one place the consensus of experts from scientific and professional psychology, education, and related fields about what constitutes ''best'' practice in the development and use of assessment devices.

It is our belief that serious problems remain in the practice of special education assessment. However, we believe with equal conviction that sound approaches to those problems are beginning to emerge. We hope that this volume points toward some of those emerging approaches.

REFERENCES

American Psychological Association. (1985). *Standards for educational and psychological testing*. Washington, D.C.: Author.

Bennett, R.E. (1983). Research and evaluation priorities for special education assessment. *Exceptional Children, 50*, 110–117.

Maher, C.A., & Bennett, R.E. (1984). *Planning and evaluating special education services*. Englewood Cliffs, NJ: Prentice-Hall.

Ysseldyke, J.E. (1983). Current practices in making psychoeducational decisions about learning disabled students. *Journal of Learning Disabilities, 16*, 226–233.

Direct and Frequent Curriculum-Based Measurement: An Alternative for Educational Decision Making

Stanley L. Deno
University of Minnesota

Douglas Marston
Minneapolis Public Schools

Gerald Tindal
University of Oregon

ABSTRACT. Direct and frequent measurement of student performance in the school curriculum is discussed as an emerging alternative way of educational decision making. Several alternative assessment models in which curriculum-based measurement is employed are discussed. To illustrate important points about curriculum-based measurement (CBM), a case example is utilized. It is seen that CBM procedures offer practical and useful means for making a range of instructional and placement decisions commonly made by special services personnel for handicapped children and youth.

Historically, efforts to measure student achievement have rested on tests created to assess performance on what could be called the "general" curriculum of the American schools rather than performance in specific school curricula. The purpose of creating and using tests based upon an analysis of what is common across school curricula is, of course, to obtain a measure of growth in skills that

The authors wish to thank the Special Education Program and staff of the Minneapolis Public Schools for their role in collecting the data presented in this paper.

Requests for reprints should be sent to: Stanley L. Deno, Department of Educational Psychology, University of Minnesota, 250 Burton Hall, 178 Pillsbury Drive, SE, Minneapolis, MN 55455.

enables general and comparative statements to be made about achievement irrespective of idiosyncrasies in local school curricula. At the same time, however, test performance on the general curriculum is typically used as a basis for making inferences about success in the specific curriculum of the local school. For example, it is not unusual for school personnel to mistakenly conclude that a student is learning what is being taught in the school's reading curriculum if the student performs well on a commercially-available reading achievement test even though the content of that test may not match well the district's reading curriculum objectives.

Whether the effort to measure achievement necessitates greater effort on the part of school personnel in selecting commercial tests that more closely match their specific school curriculum or, alternatively, specially creating tests based on that curriculum is, or should be treated as an open question. In the past fifteen years, a great deal has been written about the possibility that direct measurement of student performance in the specific curriculum used for a student's instruction can be used to reliably and validly assess achievement (c.f., Lovitt, 1967; Van Etten and Van Etten, 1976; Jenkins, Deno, & Mirkin, 1979). The viewpoint presented in this more recent literature is that technically adequate measurement procedures can be developed for use with the local school curriculum and that direct observations of performance in the curriculum not only describe progress in that specific curriculum, but also may be used to make inferences about achievement in general (Deno, Mirkin, & Chiang, 1982; Deno, Marston, & Mirkin, 1982). Further, proponents of curriculum-based measurement (CBM) procedures present the case that the data produced in this way can be more useful in making most, if not all, educational decisions because it more sensitively discriminates growth than tests created for the general curriculum. This quality is seen as important because it enables teachers to more immediately evaluate the effectiveness of their efforts to instruct a student, and to revise their approach if it is unsuccessful.

Another potential strength of CBM procedures is that they are used to repeatedly measure performance over time in school. The repeated measurements in the curriculum, then, produce time-series data revealing actual student growth over days, weeks and months that can be graphically displayed. This time-series data based on student performance in the curriculum enables teachers and other school decision makers to capitalize on two statistics—slope and variability of *individual performance*—that are unavailable when published achievement tests are used, since they are designed to be given once or twice a year. Slope and variability of individual performance can only be reliably derived from time-series data. Procedures for teacher use of slope and variability to make instructional decisions from curriculum-based performance data have been well developed (White & Haring, 1980), and are quite widely used in the field of special education. A major advantage of using slope to describe a student's rate of growth is that the effects of altering an individual student's program may be ascertained by contrasting the student's rates of growth (i.e., differing slopes) under different methods of instruction. Further, regular estimates about whether annual curriculum goals will be attained can be based on projections from individually derived slopes, and such estimates can serve as cues to change or continue a student's current program (c.f., Deno, Mirkin, & Wesson, 1984).

This paper describes several alternative assessment models that utilize curriculum-based measurement. In addition, it offers a case illustration of how CBM procedures can be used to facilitate a variety of instructional and placement decisions commonly made in special education.

ALTERNATIVE MODELS

Direct and frequent measurement of student performance in the curriculum is an approach to achievement measurement that has been used in the development of several different teaching systems in the field of special education. A brief review of some of these models is useful to clarify what are the essential features of direct and frequent CBM and how the aproach is used to create a data base for making instructional decisions. As the models are described, it is important to keep in mind that the procedures and mastery standards described are those recommended by the model developers. Our purpose here is to identify different teaching systems that capitalize on CBM and to illustrate some of the differences among them. We will not attempt to analyze the technical adequacy of the measurement procedures or the mastery standards used in each model.

Resource/Consulting Teaching and Vermont Consultant Teacher Model

The Resource Consulting Teacher Model (Idol-Maestas, 1981, 1983a, 1983b; Idol-Maestas, Lloyd, & Ritter, 1982) and the Vermont Consulting Teacher Models (Christe, McKenzie, & Burdett, 1972; Knight, Meyers, Paolucci-Whitcomb, Hasazi & Nevin, 1981; McKenzie, Egner, Knight, Perelman, Schneider, & Garvin, 1970) use a variation of the same CBM system. In this model, very specific procedures are prescribed in the assessment and placement of students in the curriculum (Idol-Maestas, 1983a; Idol-Maestas, Lloyd & Ritter, 1982). The basic measurement approach is criterion-referenced. Although procedures have been described for the use of this system in all academic areas (Idol-Maestas, 1983b), the procedures are most thoroughly detailed and developed in the area of reading. Students are measured using three random text samples at each of several grade levels, ranging from one year below estimated performance level through current grade level. A 100-word passage is used to measure rate and accuracy of reading aloud and accuracy in answering comprehension questions (factual, sequential, and inferential). A student is placed in the highest level that he or she performs with 95 percent accuracy in reading, 80 percent accuracy on the comprehension questions, and a rate of reading that exceeds various criteria established at each of several grade levels. As noted by Idol-Maestas (1983a), the accuracy criterion is similar to other criteria appearing in the literature (Fuchs, Fuchs, & Deno, 1982) though the comprehension criterion is slightly higher than the 70 percent criterion recommended by Cooper (1952) or Smith (1959). Throughout implementation of the instructional program, then, performance is monitored by determining mastery on successive 100 word passages which have been sampled from the end of the current basal story on which the student is receiving instruction. This criterion-referenced measurement of achievement, then, establishes the level of mastery in the curriculum.

In this model, achievement is measured on a daily basis. The student's rate, accuracy, and comprehension are charted on three separate equal-interval graphs, juxtaposed on one sheet of paper. A range of performance, depicted on each plot, specifies the acceptable levels for moving to the next unit in the curriculum. Although not specifically stated (Idol-Maestas, Lloyd, & Ritter, 1982) it is assumed that all three criteria must be satisfied for movement to occur. This system has been used to not only monitor effectiveness of individual student programs, but entire delivery systems, aggregating across individuals (Idol-Maestas, 1983a). The unit of measurement for this purpose was gain in criterial placement. In this study, the placement tests described above and published standardized reading tests were given to 78 students prior to, immediately following, and three months following a period of one or two years of direct reading instruction. Analysis of the results revealed gain not only in performance on both criterial placement tests but also on published reading tests. This finding provides some support for the conclusion that direct measurement of performance in the local curriculum can be used to make statements about growth in both the specific and general reading curriculum measured on published reading tests.

Directive Teaching

Stephens (1977) has described the Directive Teaching approach as "a skill training approach for individualizing instruction" in reading, arithmetic, and the area of social skills (p. 249). It includes assessment strategies, IEP objectives based on a task analysis of these areas (Stephens, Hartman & Lucas, 1978), instructional strategies for remediating skill deficits, and procedures for the measurement and evaluation of instruction (Stephens, 1977). The focus of the reading and arithmetic program is on the skills of students who have not yet attained mastery of those skills which are typically taught in kindergarten through grade three. These skills have been defined as imperative skills, "those which all children are expected to master in order to be successful in school" (Stephens, 1977, p. 252) and had been identified as appearing in at least two or more basic curriculum textbooks (of seven reviewed). Four basic steps structure the directive teaching model: assessment, planning, instruction and evaluation (Stephens, 1970, 1976).

In directive teaching, assessment and evaluation are closely related to each other, and have strong links to instruction. The measurement system utilized in directive teaching is a criterion-referenced system designed as "a survey of student functioning to determine those responses and skills that are adequate and those yet to be learned or mastered" (Stephens, 1977, p. 145). Therefore, the specific items to be taught are used as a basis for assessment.

In the actual development of the criterion-referenced measures, six steps are suggested including specification of the content to be taught, the arrangement of this content into a sequential order, the arrangement of both easier and more difficult content into a sequential order, the development of an item pool for each skill identified, and the administration of the measure to students. In addition to this development of specific items for measurement, a terminal criterion is specified and directions for administration are developed. This procedure is used for all specific tasks incorporated into instruction (Stephens, 1977). Tasks are selected for instruction that are within an appropriate range, using the following four criteria:

1. mastery, when responses are correct 100% of the time;
2. learned, when responses are correct between 90% and 99% of the time;
3. instructional, when responses are correct between 70% and 90% of the time;
4. frustration, when responses are correct less than 70% of the time.

Following a period of instruction, the criterion-referenced measures are used to evaluate the effects of instruction. These data are in turn used to determine student progress, evaluate the effectiveness of a particular instructional approach, or make instructional decisions. Though the measures are curriculum-based, this system represents a "before-and-after" treatment evaluation approach, with performance carefully documented prior to and immediately following teaching.

Exceptional Teaching and Precision Teaching

Exceptional Teaching (White & Haring, 1980), considered here to be an application of Precision Teaching (Lindsley, 1964), comprises the following components: (1) pinpointing specific behavior (referred to as "movement cycles"), (2) recording and charting of behavior on the standard behavior chart, and (3) changing instructional programs in response to outcome data.

A two stage process is used to identify and pinpoint specific behaviors for instruction. The first step is a general screening, while the second—initial assessment—is a fine-grained analysis of specific skills. The measurement tasks in these two activities consist of a series of brief (one to three minute) measurement probes repeated over ten days. In screening, the task is standardized, with two instruments suggested: Learning Screening (Koenig & Kunzelmann, 1977, 1980) or Precision Teaching Project: Screening (White & Haring, 1980). The resulting data are used to derive two types of scores: a performance score (median) and a learning score (slope).

In initial assessments, measurement probes are developed to include as many related instructional objectives as possible, ranging from elementary to more advanced items. Approximately seven to ten different probes are included, representing all academic areas. Embedded within this phase are "cue" assessments and "movement" assessments. The former includes a determination of the students' sensory preferences, whereas the latter involves documentation of requisite skills for completing the items in the probes. In summary, the purpose of screening and initial assessment is to document a student's specific academic skill strengths and deficits.

Based on screening and initial assessment results, an instructional plan is developed that is viewed as "a best guess . . . which will help this unique individual to grow" (White & Haring, 1980, p. 164). Because the philosophy of Exceptional Teaching is that "each program for each child is monitored continuously and changed immediately at the first indication that a child is not progressing as rapidly as he should" (p. 249), a data collection system which is isomorphic with that used in the initial assessment is employed. This not only ensures maximal sensitivity to performance changes but also incorporates the assessment data as baseline for evaluating program effectiveness.

The purpose of maintaining a formal monitoring program is to develop successful interventions. In this process, well-developed guidelines are used, including the development of progress standards and decision rules for changing program content. "Aimlines" are the basis for evaluating progress and are established by plotting a line on a graph from the median baseline performance to the level of performance expected (goal rate) at the program termination (goal date). This line establishes the minimum growth rate necessary for attaining the program goal. A series of decision rules are then utilized throughout program implementation to evaluate and modify instruction. The basic decision rule is as follows: If student performance falls below the aimline for three consecutive days, a change is made in the instructional program. Additionally, a change in the aimline may be warranted, although this is not a required component of the decision rule. Five different procedures are offered in the adaptation of initial aimlines: (1) "catch-up slope", using nonhandicapped peers' performance as the goal level; (2) "child-can-do-slopes", using minimum slopes obtained in at least 75% of the previous programs; (3) "similar movement-similar slope", which utilized information from comparable behavior; (4) "teacher-can-do-slope", representing teacher-established attainment and; (5) "standard celeration", based on a 25% rate of improvement over baseline. One final guideline includes the maintenance of programs until the goal is achieved, with mastery defined as performance equal to or greater than the goal level for at least one day plus an additional day for each phase change. At this point, the whole process is re-established for different skills, including initial assessment and the establishment of baseline, projection of expected levels of performance (goal date and rate), and development of aimline decision-rule criteria for evaluating the effectiveness of instruction.

Data Based Program Modification

Data Based Program Modification (Deno & Mirkin, 1977) is described as a "means of evaluating alternative solutions to the learning problems of most students encountering school difficulties" (p. 5). This system is primarily a measurement-evaluation program, with less emphasis on the content of instruction. It is based on the following five assumptions: (1) it is not currently possible to prescribe effective instructional programs for individual students, (2) special education can and must be empirically tested, (3) time-series research designs are uniquely appropriate for testing instructional changes, (4) data are needed which represent "vital signs" of educational development, and (5) professionals skilled in the analysis of time-series data are needed.

From 1977-1983, a research program was conducted through the Institute for Research on Learning Disabilities at the University of Minnesota to develop technically-adequate, curriculum-based measures for use in evaluating and modifying student programs. The results of the research supported using the following measures: in reading, the number of words read correctly from randomly-selected basal reader passages or word lists of constant difficulty in one minute (Deno, Mirkin, & Chiang, 1982); in spelling, the number of letter sequences (White & Haring, 1980) or words spelled correctly from randomly-selected curriculum (reading or spelling) word lists of constant difficulty in two minutes of dictation (Deno, Mirkin, Lowry & Kuehnle, 1980); in written expression, the number of letter sequences or words written in three minutes when given a picture stimulus or story starter. Whereas this initial research provided evidence supporting the concurrent validity of these measures, several other studies supported their predictive validity (Marston, Tindal & Deno, 1982; Marston, Mirkin & Deno, 1984), reliability (Fuchs, Deno & Marston, 1982) and sensitivity to fine gradations in growth (Deno, Marston, Lowry, Sindelar & Jenkins, 1982; Marston, Deno & Tindal, 1983; Marston, Lowry, Deno & Mirkin, 1981).

In the final section of this paper we will illustrate the use of the curriculum-based measures developed for the Data-Based Modification Model in making special education programming decisions.

CURRICULUM-BASED MEASUREMENT IN SPECIAL EDUCATION: AN ILLUSTRATION

The delivery of special education services to handicapped students involves a sequence of decisions that can, and should, be data-based. Salvia and Ysseldyke (1981) delineated five decisions that confront educators: screening, eligibility, program planning, progress monitoring, and program evaluation. What follows is a description of CBM as used by the Department of Special Education in the Minneapolis Public Schools. After outlining the development of assessment materials, a case history is provided for illustrative purposes.

Development of Measurement Materials

The first step in implementing CBM procedures is the creation of assessment tasks that are rooted in the specific academic curricula employed by the schools. Given the principle of "Least Restrictive Environment" in P.L. 94–142, the Minneapolis K-6 Resource

Program for mildly handicapped pupils began developing their measures by identifying the mainstream curriculum materials for each elementary grade level in reading, spelling, written expression and math. Since the Minneapolis reading curriculum was based on the *Ginn 720 Reading Series* (Clymer & Fenn, 1979), the resource staff identified representative passages to be read by students at each grade level. For the reading task, students were asked to read aloud from text for one minute and the number of words read correctly was then tabulated.

A similar process was followed for spelling where lists were created from words randomly drawn from each grade-level spelling curriculum. Words were then dictated for two minutes at seven second intervals. For each child the number of correct letter sequences was counted.

In math, computational facts found at each grade level of the Heath Math Curriculum were used to develop parallel math probes composed of different operations. For grades 1-3, only addition and subtraction facts were employed. However, grade 4-6 probes included addition, subtraction, multiplication and division problems. The duration of the math probe is two minutes and the number of correct digits is counted (White & Haring, 1980; Shinn & Marston, in press).

In the absence of a formal written language curriculum, Story Starters are used to assess written compositions (Deno, Marston & Mirkin, 1982). In this measurement task the child is given three minutes to write a story given a topic or leading-stimulus sentence. The number of words written correctly in the composition is then computed.

Screening

Salvia and Ysseldyke (1981) describe screening as an assessment process to "identify students who are sufficiently different from their age-mates that they require special attention" (p. 14). Since this decision is dependent upon a norm-referenced assessment, it was necessary to determine the typical performance of peers at each grade level. Marston, Mirkin and Deno (1984) contrasted a curriculum-based measurement screening system with a traditional teacher referral and identification process and concluded the two systems provided few differences in the types of pupils to be served.

Rather than use national norms for screening, local norms for Minneapolis students based upon grade-level peers were developed. The norming effort followed the Pine County Model (Tindal, Wesson, Germann, Deno & Mirkin, 1985), in which a standardization sample of over 2,000 students was used. Following this lead, the Minneapolis Special Education Department undertook the effort to establish norms for 35 elementary schools. Randomly sampling 20 students at each grade level from every school three times a year (Fall, Winter and Spring) produced a standardization sample of 7,800 pupils and provided data representing the typical or median performance on the curriculum-based measures at each grade level. The normative data were then used to establish criteria for screening teacher referrals in reading, math, spelling and written expression based on the data for each school. For all grades, a referred student who scored 50 percent lower than his or her peers on a CBM was declared eligible for further assessment (Deno & Mirkin, 1977). A case history illustrates the screening process.

Case study. Jon is a fifth grade pupil who has been having difficulties in his reading and math classes. His teacher decided in October to refer him to special education in both areas. The referral was received by the school's Special Education Resource Teacher (SERT) who conducted a three-day screening in reading and math. On each of the three days he was administered three grade-level reading passages and one math probe. At the end of the three days his median performance for each area was calculated and compared to his school grade norms as shown in Table 1. At Jon's school, a typical fifth grader in the Fall reads 110 words correctly from text; however, on the same passages Jon's number of words read correctly was 24. If Jon had read 55 or more words correctly, the screening would have indicated he was functioning at a level higher than 50% of peer performance. His median of 24, though, is less than 50% of his typical peer's performance. Thus, Jon moved to the next phase of special education assessment in reading.

A different story emerges on Jon's math performance. His median performance on the math probes is 23 correct digits whereas 44.5 is the median of his grade level peers. Jon's performance in math is 52% of the typical performance of his peers. Based on the criterion, Jon, then, is not sufficiently different from peers to be considered for further assessment in math.

School School "X"

Table 1. ACADEMIC SCREENING PEER NORMS
"Median Scores" Fall, 1983

GRADE	READING Words Correct/ Errors	SPELLING	MATH Correct Digits	WRITTEN EXPRESSION
	Ginn	Correct Letter Sequences	Mixed Probes	Total Words Correct
1	Level 4 56	47	19	-
2	Level 6 78.5	73.5	28	20.5
3	Level 8 85.5	88	24	30
4	Level 10 100.5	96	29	38.5
5	Level 11 110	93.5	44.5	43.5
6	Level 12 135.5	114	79	47

Eligibility

The second stage of the assessment process is identification or determination of eligibility. Results from criterion-validity research using CBM support the contention that the procedures reliably differentiate mildly handicapped pupils receiving special education from non-handicapped peers in reading (Deno, Mirkin & Chiang, 1982), spelling (Deno, Mirkin, Lowry & Kuehnle, 1980) and written expression (Deno, Marston & Mirkin, 1981). Subsequent research in reading documented that mildly handicapped students, pupils receiving Chapter I services, and students in regular education could be reliably classified using data generated through CBM (Marston & Deno, 1982). Shinn and Marston (in press) replicated these findings for CBM in spelling, math, and written expression and demonstrated that mildly handicapped pupils were approximately two years behind regular education peers in the school curriculum.

In Minneapolis, an eligibility for service criterion of two or more years behind in the curriculum was established. The assessment is based upon the typical range of performance for all children across the district at each grade level. Typical performance is defined as a score within one standard deviation above or below the district mean on each measure. The ranges for grades 1 to 6 on words read correctly from Ginn are presented in Figure 1. As can be seen, typical reading performance for Jon's fifth grade peers ranges from

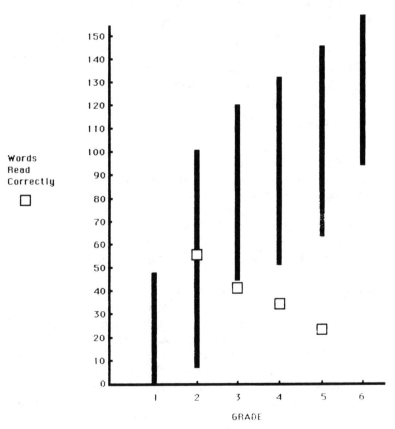

FIGURE 1. Eligibility With Curriculum-Based Measurement

62 to 145 words read correctly. Jon's 24 words read correctly is also plotted on the chart and, as may be seen, his performance falls below the typical range.

To continue Jon's eligibility assessment a "sampling back" procedure within the curriculum is initiated. Since Jon is reading below typical performance of fifth graders he is then measured three times in fourth grade reading material. His median reading performance of 36 words correct is plotted in Figure 1 and also places him below the typical range for fourth graders. Sampling back in the curriculum returns Jon to third grade Ginn material where his median performance is again determined. As shown in Figure 1 Jon read 40 words correctly, placing him at the extreme edge of the typical range. It is not until Jon reads 56 words correctly in second grade material that he falls within the typical range. At this point, with reference to the *Ginn 720* reading curriculum, Jon's performance is most similar to second graders and he is considered to be three years behind his peers. Jon is declared eligible for special education services at this point and he receives one hour of direct service daily from a SERT in reading.

Program Planning

P.L. 92-142 requires that an Individual Educational Plan (IEP) be written for each handicapped pupil that relates to the child's instructional and therapeutic needs. Further, the law prescribes that special educators set measurable goals and objectives within IEPs, and that such targets must be reviewed periodically. Typically, however, the transitions from initial assessment to a focus upon developing instructional objectives and finally to planning interventions are a problem. As Shavelson and Stern (1981) point out, teachers are more likely to plan tasks or activities to be provided in the classroom rather than describe interventions linked to objectives. Deno, Mirkin and Wesson (1983) have outlined a data-based approach to writing IEPs that incorporates the use of the curriculum measures discussed here. The form of each Long Range Goal (LRG) is the same including the stimulus condition, the academic *behavior* to be observed and recorded, and the *criterion* levels of behavior representing the goal. These components are shown in Figure 2 and together constitute the IEP goal. The system is used in the Minneapolis School-Based Resource Program and aids in the program planning process.

	Condition	Behavior	Criteria
Reading	In _____ (total # weeks until next review) when presented with stories from Level _____ (level # in which the student currently reads 55-78 wpm) in _____ (name of reading series)	student will read aloud	90-150 words correctly with 7 errors or fewer (The team should choose a specific criterion from within this range.)
Spelling	In _____ (total # weeks until next annual review) when dictated words for 2 minutes from Level ___ (level in which student currently spells 20-39 letter sequences correct (1sc) for Grades 1 & 2 or 40-59 letter sequences correct (Grades 3-6)	student will spell words	(60-80) 1sc (for Grades 1 & 2) or (80-140) 1sc (for Grades 3-6).
Written Expression	In _____ (total # weeks until next annual review) when presented with a story starter or topic sentence and three minutes in which to write a story	student will write	a total of _____ (words or letter sequences correct -see Table 7-1)
Math	In _____ (total # weeks until next annual review) when given a copy of math facts at level ___ and two minutes in which to work.	student will write	_____ digits correct.

FIGURE 2. Long-Range Goal Planning Chart for Writing IEP's.

In Jon's case where he has read 56 words correctly, the sampling back procedure fixed his LRG material at the second grade level. The criterion selected by the SERT for goal attainment was 100 words read correctly, with fewer than five errors, on the LRG material which is a second grade basal text. The SERT then instructs and measures progress toward the LRG to evaluate the effectiveness of that instruction.

Progress Monitoring

The fourth assessment area identified by Salvia and Ysseldyke (1981) is that of monitoring student progress. Traditionally, such an assessment has been conducted informally by teachers or has involved the use of commercially-available achievement tests. Such practice, however, is problematic for several reasons. First, the reliability and validity of teacher-made tests is usually unknown, and for that reason their use to make important progress decisions is indefensible. Second, commercially-developed tests are usually used in a pre and posttest evaluation design to describe gains. Use of pre-posttest designs for measuring educational change has been questioned (Cronbach & Furby, 1970). Third, the content of many standardized achievement tests does not necessarily match the particular curriculum used to teach the student (Jenkins & Pany, 1978; Eaton & Lovitt, 1972). Finally, Carver (1974) argues that most standardized achievement tests were not designed primarily to measure learning or change in student performance.

A viable alternative is to use CBM to create a time-series research design. The feasibility of such an alternative was demonstrated by Marston and Deno (1982) who contrasted the sensitivity of commercially-prepared reading tests and CBM to measure student growth. Their data revealed that CBM procedures were sensitive to growth in student performance over a 16 week period while the commercial tests were not.

To return to our case illustration, Jon was declared eligible for service in reading at the end of October. At that time, a progress monitoring system was implemented in which his reading proficiency was measured three times a week in his long range goal material. These data are graphed in Figure 3. A review of the performance graph shows his baseline level of 56 words with a goal 25 weeks later of 100. Connecting baseline level and the IEP goal is Jon's aimline, a projected line of improvement to which Jon must adhere if he is to accomplish his reading goal. Because Jon is trying to achieve a 44 word improvement in reading over a 22 week period, the goal-based improvement line increases at a slope of 2.0 words per week. In Figure 3 we observe that in the first three weeks of SERT intervention Jon was making little progress toward his goal and was below his goal line. Utilizing the "Split-Middle Technique" (White & Haring, 1980) for drawing trend lines reveals that Jon was growing about one half of a word per week in reading.

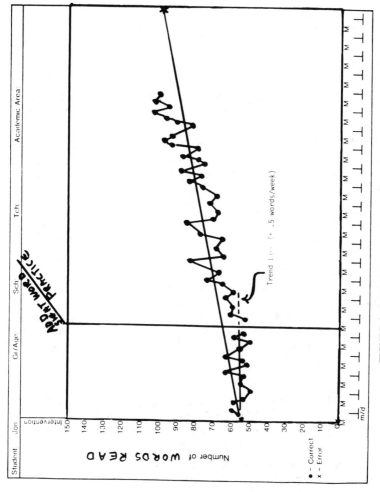

FIGURE 3. Jon's Performance Graph in Reading

21

Projection of this trend line reveals that Jon would not attain his LRG and indicates a change in teaching strategies is necessary for greater improvement. In this case Jon's SERT added sight word drill and noted this on the graph with an "intervention line" drawn in on the first day of implementation. Thereafter, a dramatic improvement is noted on his reading graph and his IEP reading goal is attained five weeks before the target date.

Program Evaluation

Salvia and Ysseldyke (1981) describe program evaluation as an assessment of overall program effectiveness. Usually such a judgment is made at a group rather than individual level. With the data-based programming system in place in Minneapolis, program evaluation can be easily conducted. The use of a common database facilitates the aggregation of data across individual students and SERTS, and increases the probability of making generalizations about programmatic issues.

Figure 4 illustrates one example of how the CBM data might be used by an adminstrator to review and evaluate placement criteria. The reading performance of four different types of students is plotted across grades 1–6. As can be seen, the typical performance of elementary pupils placed in regular education is highest and is significantly better than those pupils receiving Chapter I services. At the same time, the performance of the Chapter I pupils and students referred for special education, but not determined eligible, is not significantly different. Finally, the differences between children referred and placed or not placed in special education is observably and statistically significant. Given that a common set of student outcome data is collected across these four types of groups, the administrator can begin viewing the placement process objectively.

The common database, with its emphasis on repeated measurement also provides the administrator with the opportunity for reviewing aggregated progress data for all students. In the school-based resource program the average slope of improvement on IEP reading goals was calculated at each grade level. As may be seen in Table 2, average growth ranged from .60 words per week at sixth grade to 1.46 words per week at second grade. Such data, when compared to other placement groups demonstrates to the administrator the degree of effectiveness of programs being implemented by special services.

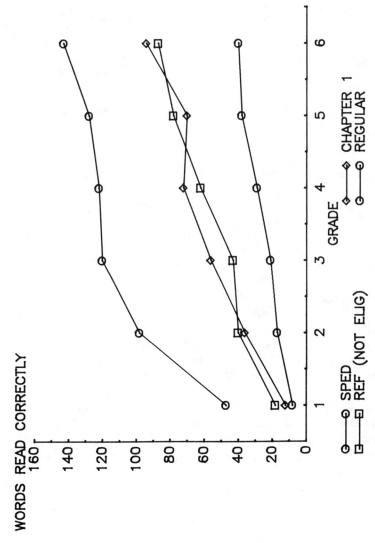

FIGURE 4. Comparative Performance of Regular Class, Chapter 1, Referred and Special Education Students on the Curriculum-Based Reading Measure

Table 2

Average Number of Words Increased Each Week on IEP Reading Goals

Grade	N	Mean	Standard Deviation
1	24	1.31	.90
2	58	1.46	1.03
3	84	1.19	1.87
4	57	1.30	.96
5	41	1.26	.95
6	31	.60	1.67

CONCLUSION

In this paper we have attempted to present direct and frequent curriculum-based measurement (CBM) as an alternative model for assessment and programming in special education. The reasons for using CBM were briefly considered and alternative intervention models incorporating some form of CBM were described. Finally, the use of the Data Based Program Modification Model in special education was illustrated by presenting the Minneapolis Public School's System for School-Based Services in Grades K–6.

We hope that the reader is persuaded that the developments occurring with direct and frequent CBM are sufficiently promising to take a closer look. Our own experience leads us to conclude that using CBM in data-based programming is not only technically feasible and logically defensible, but also produces better services for individual students.

REFERENCES

Carver, R.P. (1974). Two dimensions of tests: Psychometric and edumetric. *American Psychologist, 29*, 512–518.

Christie, L., McKenzie, H., & Burdett, C. (1972). The consulting teacher approach to special education: Inservice training for regular classroom teachers. *Focus on Exceptional Children, 5*, 1–10.

Clymer, T., & Fenn, T. (1979). *Reading 720 rainbow edition.* Lexington, MA: Ginn.

Cooper, J.L. (1952). The effect of adjustment of basal reading materials in reading achievement. Unpublished doctoral dissertation, Boston University.

Cronbach, L.J., & Furby, L. (1970). How we should measure "change"—or should we? *Psychological Bulletin, 74*, 68–80.

Deno, S., Chiang, B., Tindal, G., & Blackburn, M. (1979). *Experimental analysis of program components: An approach to research in CSDCs* (Research Report No. 12). Minneapolis, MN: University of Minnesota, Institute for Research on Learning Disabilities.

Deno, S., Marston, D., & Mirkin, P. (1982). Valid measurement procedures for continuous evaluation of written expression. *Exceptional Children, 48*(4), 368–371.

Deno, S. Marston, D., Mirkin, P., Lowry, L., Sindelar, P., & Jenkins, J. (1982). *The use of standard tasks to measure achievement in reading, spelling, and written expression: A normative and developmental study* (Research Report No. 87). Minneapolis, MN: University of Minnesota, Institute for Research on Learning Disabilities. (ERIC Document Reproduction Service No. ED 227 129).

Deno, S., & Mirkin, P. (1977). *Data-based program modification: A manual.* Minneapolis, MN: Leadership Training Institute/Special Education, University of Minnesota.

Deno, S., Mirkin, P.K., & Chiang, B. (1982). Identifying valid measures of reading. *Exceptional Children, 49*(1), 36–45.

Deno, S., Mirkin P., Lowry, L., & Kuehnle, K. (1980). *Relationships among simple measures of spelling and performance on standardized achievement tests.* (Research Report No. 21). Minneapolis, MN: University of Minnesota, Institute for Research on Learning Disabilities. (ERIC Document Reproduction Service No. ED 197 508).

Deno, S.L., Mirkin, P.K., & Wesson, C. (1984). How to write effective data-based IEPs. *Teaching Exceptional Children, 16*(2), 99–104.

Eaton, M., & Lovitt, T. (1972). Achievement tests vs. direct and daily measurement. In G. Semb (Ed.) *Behavior analysis and education.* Lawrence, KS: University of Kansas.

Englemann, S., & Brunner, E. (1974). *DISTAR reading level one.* Chicago: Science Research Associates.

Fuchs, L., Deno, S., & Marston, D. (1982). *Use of aggregation to improve the reliability of simple direct measures of academic performance* (Research Report No. 94). Minneapolis, MN: Institute for Research on Learning Disabilities.

Fuchs, L.S., Deno, S.L., & Roettger, A. (1983). *The effect of alternative data-utilization rules on spelling achievement: An N of 1 study* (Research Report No. 120). Minneapolis, MN: University of Minnesota, Institute for Research on Learning Disabilities. (ERIC Document Reproduction Service No. ED 236 844).

Fuchs, L., Fuchs, D., & Deno, S. (1982). Reliability and validity of curriculum-based informal reading inventories. *Reading Research Quarterly, 18*(1), 6–25.

Germann, G., & Tindal, G. (1983). (Summary report for Pine County Cooperative: 1982–1983). Unpublished raw data.

Idol-Maestas, L. (1981). A teacher training model: The resource consulting teacher. *Behavioral Disorders, 6*(2), 108–121.

Idol-Maestas, L. (1983a). *A follow-up report on mildly handicapped students receiving direct reading instruction.* Unpublished manuscript.

Idol-Maestas, L. (1983b). *Special educator's consultation handbook.* Rockville, MD: Aspen Publications.

Idol-Maestas, L., Lloyd, S., & Ritter, S. (1982). *A model for direct, data based reading instruction.* Champaign, IL: Department of Special Education, (ERIC Reproduction Service No. ED 219 738).

Jenkins, J.R., Deno, S.L. & Mirkin, P.K. (1979). Measuring pupil progress toward the least restrictive environment. *Learning Disabilities Quarterly, 2*(4), 81–92.

Jenkins, J., & Pany, D. (1978). Standardized achievement tests: How useful for special education? *Exceptional Children, 44*, 448–453.

Knight, M., Meyers, H., Paolucci-Whitcomb, P., Hasazi, S., & Nevin, A. (1981). A four year evaluation for consulting teacher service. *Behavior Disorders, 6*(2), 92–100.

Koenig, C., & Kunzelman, H. (1977). *Learning screening.* Kansas City, MO: International Management Systems.

Koenig, C., & Kunzelman, H. (1980). *Classroom learning screening.* Columbus, OH: Charles E. Merrill Publishing Company.

Lakin, K.C. (1983). A response to Gene V. Glass. *Policy Studies Review, 2*(1), 233–240.

Leinhardt, G., & Pallay, A. (1982). Restrictive educational settings: Exile or haven. *Review of Educational Research, 52*(4), 557–578.

Lindsley, O.R. (1964). Direct measurement and prothesis of retarded behavior. *Journal of Education, 147,* 62–81.

Lovitt, T.C. (1967). Assessment of children with learning disabilities. *Exceptional Children, 34*(4), 233–239.

Lovitt, T., & Hansen, C. (1976). Round 1: Placing the child in the right reader. *Journal of Learning Disabilities, 9*(6), 18–24.

Marston, D., & Deno, S.L. (1982). *Implementation of direct and repeated measurement in the school setting* (Research Report No. 106). Minneapolis, MN: University of Minnesota, Institute for Research on Learning Disabilities.

Marston, D., Deno, S., & Tindal, G. (1983). *A comparison of standardized achievement tests and direct measurement techniques in measuring pupil progress* (Research Report No. 126). Minneapolis, MN: University of Minnesota, Institute for Research on Learning Disabilities.

Marston, D., Lowry, L., Deno, S., & Mirkin, P. (1981). *An analysis of learning trends in simple measures of reading, spelling, and written expression; A longitudinal study* (Research Report No. 49). Minneapolis, MN: University of Minnesota, Institute for Research on Learning Disabilities.

Marston, D., Mirkin, P.K., & Deno, S.L. (1984). Curriculum-based measurement: An alternative to traditional referral, screening and identification. *Journal of Special Education, 18*(2), 109–118.

Marston, D., Tindal, G., & Deno, S. (1982). *Predictive efficiency of direct, repeated measurement: An analysis of cost and accuracy in classification* (Research Report No. 104). Minneapolis, MN: University of Minnesota, Institute for Research on Learning Disabilities.

Marston, D., Tindal, G., & Deno, S. (1984). Eligibility for learning disability services: A direct and repeated measurement approach. *Exceptional Children, 6,* 544–555.

McKenzie, H., Egner, A., Knight, M., Perelman, P., Schnieder, B., & Garvin, J. (1970). Training consulting teachers to assist elementary teachers in the management and education of handicapped children. *Exceptional Children, 37,* 137–143.

Salvia, J., & Ysseldyke, J. (1981). *Assessment in special and remedial education* (2nd ed.). Boston: Houghton-Mifflen.

Shavelson, R., & Stern, P. (1981). Research on teachers' pedagogical thoughts, judgments, decisions, and behavior. *Review of Educational Research, 51,* 455–498.

Shinn, M., & Marston, D. (In press). Assessing mildly handicapped, low achieving and regular education students: A curriculum based approach. *Remedial and Special Education.*

Smith, N.B. (1959). *Graded selections for informal reading diagnosis.* New York: New York University Press.

Stephens, T. (1970). *Directive teaching of children with learning and behavioral handicaps.* Columbus, OH: Charles E. Merrill Publishing Company.

Stephens, T. (1976). *Directive teaching of children with learning and behavioral handicaps* (2nd ed.). Columbus, OH Charles E. Merrill Publishing Company.

Stephens, T. (1977). *Teaching skills to children with learning and behavior disorders.* Columbus, OH: Charles E. Merrill Publishing Company.

Stephens, T., Hartman, & Lucas. (1978). *Teaching children basic skills: A curriculum handbook.* Columbus, OH: Charles E. Merrill Publishing Company.

Tindal, G., Wesson, C., Germann, G., Deno, S., & Mirkin, P. (1985). The Pine County model for special education delivery: A data-based system. In T. Kratochwill (Ed.) *Advances in school psychology:* vol. 4 Hillsdale. NJ: Lawrence Earlbaum.

Van Etten, C., & Van Etten, G. (1976). The measurement of pupil progress and selecting instructional materials. *Journal of Learning Disabilities, 9*(8), 469–480.

Wesson, C., Deno, S., Mirkin, P., Sevik, B., Skiba, R., King, R., Tindal, G., & Maruyama, G. (1982). *Teaching structure and student achievement effects of curriculum-based measurement: A casual (structural) analysis* (Research Report No. 105). Minneapolis, MN: University of Minnesota, Institute for Research on Learning Disabilities. (ERIC Document Reproduction Service No. ED 227 127).

Wesson, C., Skiba, R., Sevcik, B., King, R., Tindal, G., Mirkin, P., & Deno, S. (1983) *The impact of structure of instruction and the use of technically adequate instructional data on reading improvement* (Research Report No. 116). Minneapolis, MN: Institute for Research on Learning Disabilities.

White, O., & Haring, N. (1980). *Exceptional Teaching,* Columbus, OH: Charles E. Merrill Publishing Company.

Path-Referenced Assessment: A Guide for Instructional Management

John R. Bergan

University of Arizona

ABSTRACT. Path-referenced assessment is considered as an innovative attempt to move closer to the sought-after goal of making assessment directly relevant to instructional concerns of all learners including the handicapped. The technology of this rapidly developing form of assessment allows determinations to be made about educational progress of learners resulting from instruction. In this article, the nature of path-referenced assessment is described, its relationship to instructional management is delineated, and how path-referenced assessment relates to adaptive measurement systems is considered.

The principal function of assessment in the contemporary school is gathering information on student performance for purposes of instructional management. Assessment provides the foundation for a broad range of management decisions. Familiar examples include decisions involving instructional program evaluation, educational placement, and the diagnosis of learner needs. The schools have sought three kinds of information from assessment programs: information on the relative standing of students in norm groups, information about the specific instructional objectives that students have mastered, and information about the progress that students have made as a result of instruction. Norm-referenced assessment has provided the schools with information about relative standing. Criterion-referenced assessment has afforded information about the

The development of this paper has been funded in part by the Department of Health and Human Services under Contract No. HHS-105-81-C-008. The contents of this publication do not necessarily reflect the views or policies of the Department of Health and Human Services, nor does mention of trade names, commercial products, or organizations imply endorsement by the U.S. Government.

Requests for reprints should be sent to: John R. Bergan, Department of Educational Psychology, University of Arizona, Tucson, AZ 85721.

29

mastery of objectives. Unfortunately, until recently there has been no adequate procedure for assessing student progress. Path-rcferenced assessment was established to provide an effective way to determine progress along paths reflecting development.

THE NATURE OF PATH-REFERENCED ASSESSMENT

Path-referenced assessment implies a developmental perspective about the nature of competence. The path-referenced approach assumes sequential changes in capability reflecting a movement from simple to more complex capabilities. Path-referenced assessment also reflects a point of view regarding the manner in which examinee test performance is defined. More specifically, in the path-referenced approach, examinee performance is described in terms of position achieved along various paths to development.

The technology for path-referenced assessment evolved over a period of years in connection with the development of the *Head Start Measures Battery* (Bergan & Smith, 1984), a set of path-referenced assessment instruments developed for use in program management in the Head Start organization. The *Head Start Measures Battery* includes measures in six content areas: language, math, nature and science, perception, reading, and social development. The Battery was developed under a contract from the Administration for Children, Youth, and Families in the U.S. Department of Health and Human Services to the University of Arizona. Work on some of the scales was done under subcontract to the University of California at Santa Cruz and Indiana University. The Battery is currently being used in over 190 Head Start programs with aproximately 19,000 children.

Path-Referenced Assessment Defined

It is customary to define types of assessment in terms of the manner in which student performance is referenced. Norm-referenced assessment indicates a student's relative position in a norm group. The norm-referenced approach is useful for answering questions about the relative standing of individuals, classes, or schools in an appropriate reference group. Criterion-referenced assessment links student performance to criteria defined by specific instructional objectives. Criterion-referenced assessment is useful for determining the specific skills mastered by students. Path-referenced assessment describes student progress along empirically-validated developmental paths reflecting the achievement of educational objectives. Path-referenced assessment generates information about educational progress that cannot be gained in other ways. The path-referenced approach identifies the position of individuals, or groups in a developmental sequence, and determines changes in position that can be attributed to instruction. The unique feature of path-referencing is that it provides quantitative scales for measuring educational progress that are linked to validated developmental sequences. The path-referenced approach affords the information available from a criterion-referenced test plus information on path position and path progress. Moreover, path-referenced assessment can be linked to norm-referenced technology to produce information on position in a norm group.

Path-Referenced Assessment and Latent Trait Technology

Concern for learning sequences is not new in education. For example, many criterion-referenced assessment programs make some assumptions about the sequencing of learning tasks (Glaser & Nitko, 1971; Nitko, 1980). In the criterion-referenced approach, sets of learning tasks are organized into hypothesized hierarchies in which tasks placed at low levels in a hierarchy are assumed to be prerequisite to tasks placed at high levels. During the early days of criterion-referenced assessment, attempts were made to validate learning sequences empirically. However, adequate technology was not available to carry out such validation (Bergan, 1980). As criterion-referenced assessment evolved, efforts to achieve sequence validation were largely abandoned. Moreover, assumptions about sequencing, which were once an important characteristic of criterion-referenced tests, tended to play only a minimal role in the development of criterion-referenced instruments.

Path-referenced assessment shares the early concern of criterion-referenced assessment with the issue of sequential learning. However, the path-referenced approach is based on a general latent trait model (see, for example, Bock & Aitkin, 1981; Lord, 1980), which includes assumptions about the factors affecting task performance that are quite different from those underlying criterion-referenced assessment. The general latent trait model holds that the probability of accurate task performance is a function of a latent (unobserved) ability and of task characterisitcs (e.g., Lord, 1980). One characteristic, task difficulty, is particularly important for path-referenced assessment. Within the path-referenced approach, variations in task difficulty are used as a basis for constructing sequences reflecting paths of learning and development. Bergan (1985) has developed variations of the general latent trait model making it possible to test the hypothesis that tasks vary in difficulty level. Hypothesis testing provides the basis for establishing empirically validated sequences or paths of learning and development.

Within the latent trait model, ability and difficulty are quantified on the same scale. As a result, an individual's ability score serves as an indicator of developmental level or path position. That is, the ability score indicates the position of the individual in a developmental sequence. Information on path position is highly useful in planning instruction for the individual. Knowledge of path position indicates what the individual has mastered in the past and the challenges that lie ahead as development progresses.

The latent trait technology underlying path-referenced assessment is useful in several ways. Latent trait techniques make it possible to:

1. test assumptions about the sequencing of learning tasks,
2. measure progress along developmental paths on a continuous scale,
3. measure developmental gains resulting from instruction,
4. place sequences across grade levels on a common scale assessing long-range development,
5. provide an adaptive measurement system capable of accommodating a changing curriculum. (Curriculum changes may require changes in skills targeted for evaluation. Path-referenced assessment can place scores from old and new versions of a test on a common scale so that achievement scores can be compared across years even during those times when the curriculum is undergoing modification.)

PATH REFERENCED ASSESSMENT AND INSTRUCTIONAL MANAGEMENT

Path-referenced assessment is intended to serve as a tool for the management of instruction. Path-referenced technology provides a perspective that links educational decisions to information about the organization and patterning of change in student knowledge. In the path-referenced approach, information about current student status is tied both to possible future achievement and to past accomplishment in order to facilitate the assessment of change. This dynamic view relates educational decision making to the fundamental goal of enhancing student progress.

The path-referenced approach can be used by teachers and students to make instructional management decisions in the classroom. For instance, path-referenced assessment technology can be employed to guide the individualization of instruction. Likewise, path-referenced assessment can be applied by school administrators for purposes of program evaluation. For example, path-referenced techniques could be employed by a school district to determine the amount of educational progress that could be attributed to instruction afforded in an innovative educational program.

Management and the Path-Referenced Focus on Dynamics

The path-referenced perspective provides a dynamic view of student competence focusing on changes in capability occurring over varying time periods. Change is viewed as reflecting continuous progress along paths of development. Recognition of continuous change makes it possible to measure educational progress on a quantitative scale.

The path-referenced point of view assumes that progress in the acquisition of knowledge occurs in organized patterns in which more complex forms of competence are built upon simpler forms. These patterns are depicted in terms of paths of development. Path-referenced assessment technology is designed to validate assumptions about changes in student knowledge empirically. Empirical validation provides the instructional manager with concrete information on changes in student knowledge. This kind of information can be used not only to guide the long-range assessment of student progress, but also to direct long-range curriculum planning.

The focus on change characteristic of path-referenced assessment stands in marked contrast to the emphasis on current status reflected in both norm-referenced and criterion-referenced assessment. Path-referenced assessment is also concerned with status. However, status is conceptualized in a different way. In norm-referenced assessment, status is defined by relative position in a norm group. In criterion-referenced assessment, status is defined by the proportion of skills mastered in a well-defined domain. From the path-referenced point of view, status is a set of current positions along paths to development. These positions reflect the culmination of past learning and the beginning of future learning.

The link to the past and to the future inherent in the path-referenced conception of status has important implications for the educational decision-maker. The determination of current status in terms of path position implies the mastery of specific subordinate competencies. The instructional decision maker who knows what has been learned is in a better position to determine what should be taught than the decision maker who does not have this kind of information. The path-referenced determination of status also implies a direction for future learning. This direction affords precise information to guide the selection of future learning objectives.

Path-Referenced Decision-Making Information

Path-referenced assessment provides two types of information to the instructional manager. The first of these is information on what the student has accomplished at various points in the instructional process. Path-referenced test items, like criterion-referenced test items, are designed to be linked directly to the mastery of instructional objectives. The results of a path-referenced assessment communicate to the instructional decision-maker those objectives that have been mastered and those objectives that have not been mastered. The advantages associated with this type of information are well documented in the literature on criterion-referenced assessment (e.g., Hambleton, 1980; Popham, 1978). In brief, linking assessment to the mastery of objectives relates measurement directly to instruction. What is tested is based on what is supposed to be taught. Moreover, what has been accomplished by learners is communicated in an unambiguous way to instructional managers, thus facilitating instructional planning decisions.

The second type of information generated in path-referenced assessment is quantitative information about path position. The application of latent trait techniques makes it possible to place test items reflecting paths of development on a continuous scale that can be used to quantify path position. Quantitative information on path position makes it possible to quantify the amount of change that has taken place as a result of instruction. Information of this kind provides an unambiguous quantitative index that can be used to assess the effects of instructional programs.

Management Decisions in Path-Referenced Assessment

Path-referenced assessment provides information that can be used in making a variety of types of instructional decisions. These decisions relate to four types of management activity; individualizing instruction in the classroom, placing children in special programs, planning and designing curricula, and evaluating instructional programs.

Information on the mastery of objectives linked to information on path position provides the instructional manager (teacher) with an empirical basis for individualizing instruction in the classroom. The manager not only is given a detailed account of what the student knows, but also is apprised of the implications of that knowledge for both past and future learning. Information of this kind affords the basis for placing the student at the appropriate position in an instructional sequence and for monitoring progress through the sequence.

Placement of students in special programs is generally accomplished through the application of norm-referenced assessment. However, path-referenced assessment may also provide useful information for placement decisions. The general goal of special placement is to provide a program that is appropriate to the learning needs of the student. Path-referenced assessment affords information of direct relevance to this purpose. The path-referenced approach to placement decisions involves matching information on path position and progress to information on the learning opportunities available in specific instructional programs. A decision to place would imply that instruction congruent with the student's path position could be better provided in the special program than in other available alternatives.

Information on developmental sequences afforded in path-referenced assessment offers an empirical basis for the planning and design of curricula. Path-referenced technology produces empirically validated sequences reflecting changes in capability occurring over long time spans. These sequences can be used as a basis for designing curricular sequences.

Path-referenced assessment can also be used in the evaluation of instructional programs. A fundamental question often raised in program evaluation is that of determining changes in competence that can be attributed to instruction. Path-referenced assessment is designed to produce information about change that cannot be gained in other ways. This fact is best illustrated by comparing path-referenced change scores to the techniques typically used to reflect change in program evaluation. The technology generally used in program evaluation relies heavily on concepts of expected normal growth as reflected in indices such as the grade equivalent score (Linn, 1981). Statements asserting that children gained so many months in reading or math are commonplace in program evaluation reports. Criticisms of the grade-equivalent score are widespread in the measurement and evaluation literature (e.g., Angoff, 1971; Horst, 1976; Linn, 1981; Linn & Slinde, 1977). Other norm-referenced indices used to assess change (e.g., the percentile rank and the normal curve equivalent) are also fraught with problems (Linn, 1981).

A fundamental problem with such norm-referenced change indices as age and grade equivalents is that below-average, average, and above-average students can be expected to grow at different rates to maintain their relative standing in the norm group (Linn, 1981). Accordingly, a given amount of gain must be interpreted differently for students of different ability levels.

Another serious problem with these scores is that the same score may mean different things for students at different grade levels (Angoff, 1971). For example, a third grader who achieves a grade-equivalent score of 3.0 may have markedly different skills than a fifth grader who achieves the identical score. As this example shows, the grade-equivalent score is not useful in identifying the specific skills that students have learned as a result of instruction. Advocates of criterion-referenced assessment (e.g., Popham, 1978) have argued persuasively that the specification of skills mastered as a result of instruction is fundamental to effective program evaluation.

The indices of change provided in path-referenced assessment avoid the problems associated with these commonly used norm-referenced indices. The scales of continuous progress generated through path-referenced assessment are not linked to the relative position of a student in a norm group. Thus, progress measured in terms of path-referenced scales can be interpreted unequivocally for superior, average, and below-average students. Likewise, both quantitative and qualitative indices of path position provide an unambiguous link to the mastery of specific skills. Thus, if two students have the same path position score, it can be assumed that for the particular path they possess similar skills. More generally, knowledge of any particular path-position score can be taken as an indicator of the kinds of skills possessed by the student.

The application of path-referenced assessment technology allows the program manager to ask and to receive a meaningful answer to the fundamental question of how much students have learned as a result of instruction. In addition, path-referenced assessment technology makes it possible to link quantitative information on the extent of student progress to the specific skills mastered in the instructional process. This kind of information not only makes it possible to evaluate the effectiveness of an instructional program, but also to pinpoint specific areas of program strength and weakness so that corrective action may be taken where required. The linking of the quantity of learning to the content of learning offers the opportunity to identify the specific competencies that are and are not being taught in an instructional program and to anticipate the potential impact of emphasizing or deemphasizing any particular set of competencies on overall learning outcomes.

ADAPTIVE MEASUREMENT

In order for path-referenced assessment to meet the needs of a changing, pluralistic society, it is useful to link this technology to adaptive measurement systems. The phrase *adaptive measurement system* is used to indicate the requirement of developing an integrated set of measurement techniques including measuring instruments, statistical techniques, and computer software that can be applied to continuously adapt measuring instruments to the changing needs of diverse educational programs.

Rationale for Adaptive Measurement

There are several reasons for using an adaptive measurement system rather than a set of packaged tests. The first of these has to do with the rapid advances that are occurring in the production of the scientific knowledge based on human development. Effective measurement requires the capability of incorporating new information about development into the measurement process.

A second justification for an adaptive system involves societal change and accompanying curricular change. Rapid social and educational change is a close concommitant of scientific advancement. Educational curricula undergo frequent change in contemporary schools. Measures which cannot adapt to these changes run the risk of becoming quickly outdated.

A third reason for establishing an adaptive measurement system involves the generalizability of test results. Measurement instruments are typically assumed to assess generalized skills rather than performance on a specific set of test items. If assessment is organized in terms of a specific set of test items, there is a danger that instruction will focus on teaching the test rather than the underlying skills that the test is designed to measure. To avoid this problem, an adaptive measurement system can be designed to construct tests from an item bank (see, for example, Millman & Arter, 1984) containing large numbers of items defining an item population representing the skills targeted for instruction.

A fourth reason for an adaptive measurement system has to do with the problem of accommodating cultural diversity. Educational programs in contemporary America must accommodate students from many different ethnic and linguistic backgrounds. The effective measurement of educational progress requires adaptation to the extensive diversity that exists among the population of school children. Packaged assessment devices cannot adequately accommodate the existing diversity. For example, linguistic diversity in Head Start includes not only several varieties of Spanish, but also French, Chinese, and a host of other languages. As people from other lands continue to immigrate into the United States, the challenge of accommodating ethnic and linguistic diversity will increase. Measures that can be adapted to the unique needs of different ethnic groups are required if educational progress is to be assessed adequately in these groups.

A fifth justification for an adaptive measurement system involves variations in local program needs. The content of educational programs differ markedly from one setting to another. Assessment devices used both in diagnosis and in program evaluation should take local program objectives and characteristics into account. Accommodating local needs calls for an adaptive system that can be altered to meet varying local conditions.

The Head Start Measurement System

In order to meet measurement needs in Head Start, The University of Arizona has developed an adaptive measurement system for the Head Start organization. The system contains three major features. First, it includes a set of procedures for staying abreast of advances in the scientific knowledge base and for incorporating significant new findings into the measurement process. Content specialists with knowledge not only of the subject matter field in question, but also of the psychological processes manifested by children interacting with the content of interest are responsible for linking advances in the scientific knowledge base to measures of development. The modification of measurement instruments based on new information from the scientific knowledge base is being subjected to content validation through examinations of the technical quality of the items and of the extent to which the items adequately represent the content area under examination.

The second feature of the system is a set of procedures for incorporating new items into the measures provided for educational programs. Item banking involving database technology (Ullman, 1982) and the application of latent trait techniques is being used for this purpose (Stocking & Lord, 1983). The strategy of developing an item bank from which different tests may be constructed rather than a set of specific tests provides the measurement system with the necessary flexibility to accommodate diverse local programs and changing societal needs. Latent trait statistical procedures play a key role in establishing an item bank. Latent trait techniques make is possible to place old items and new items on a common scale. This feature of latent trait technology affords the opportunity of revising measures as required to meet changing educational needs.

The third feature of the system is a set of procedures for obtaining input from local programs regarding the kinds of things that they would like to see in the assessment instruments that they use. A ''hot line'' is used with a toll free number that local Head Start sites can use to contact the Center for Educational Evaluation and Measurement to indicate any problems that they may be having implementing the Measures program. In addition, reporting forms are used to obtain input from local programs to aid in constructing future versions of the measuring instruments. The reporting forms deal not only with the kinds of skills that programs would like to have included in the measures, but also with a variety of practical concerns related to assessment. For example, input is sought on the amount of time available for assessment and the amount of time required for assessment.

CONCLUSION

The path-referenced assessment system represents an attempt to move closer to the long-held goal of making assessment directly relevant to instructional concerns. Path-referenced assessment technology makes it possible to focus assessment on the fundamental question of determining educational progress resulting from instruction. The incorporation of path-referenced technology into a measurement system affords the possibility of adapting that technology to the varied needs of diverse and changing educational programs.

REFERENCES

Angoff, W.H. (1971). Scales, norms and equivalent scores. In R.L. Thorndike *Educational Measurement*. (2nd ed.) Washington, D.C.: American Council of Education, pp. 508–600.

Bergan, J.R. (April, 1985). *Restricted item response models for developmental assessment.* Paper presented at annual meeting of American Educational Research Association, Chicago, Illinois.

Bergan, J.R. (1980). The structural analysis of behavior; An alternative to the learning hierarchy model. *Review of Educational Research, 50*, pp. 625–646.

Bergan, J.R. (Ed.) & Smith, A.N. (Government Project Officer) (1984). *Head Start Measures Battery*. Tests developed for The Administration for Children, Youth, and Families, Department of Health & Human Services under Contract No. HHS-105-81-C-008.

Bock, R.D., & Aitkin, M. (1981). Marginal maximum likelihood estimation of item parameters; Application of an EM algorithm. *Psychometrika, 46*, 433–459.

Glaser, R., & Nitko, A.J. (1971). Measurement in learning and instruction. In R.L. Thorndike (Ed.) *Educational Measurement* (2nd ed.) Washington, D.C.: American Council of Education.

Hambleton, R.K. (1980). Test score validity for standard setting methods. In R.A. Berk (Ed.), *Criterion-referenced measurement: The state of the art*.

Horst, D.T. (1976). *What's bad about grade equivalent score E.S.E.A.: Title I evaluation & report*. System Technical Report 1, Mountain View, Ca. RMC Corp.

Linn, R. (1981). Measuring pretest/posttest performance change. In R.A. Berk (Ed.), *Educational evaluation methodology: The state of the art*. Baltimore: Johns Hopkins University Press.

Linn, R., & Slinde, J.A. (1977). The determination of the significance of change between pre & post test period. *Review of Educational Research, 47* 121–150.

Lord, F. (1980). *Applications of item response theory to practical testing problems*. Hillsdale, N.J.: Lawrence Erlbaum Associates.

Millman, J., & Arter, J.A. (1984). Issues in item banking. *Journal of Educational Measurement*, *21*, pp. 315–330.

Nitko, A. (1980). Distinguishing the many varieties of criterion referenced tests. *Review of Educational Research*, *50*, 461–485.

Pelavin, S. & Barker, P. (February, 1976). *A study of the generalizability of the results of a standardized achievement test*. W.M.-9234-NIE. Santa Monica: Rand Corp.

Popham, W.J. (1978). *Criterion-referenced assessment*. Englewood Cliffs, N.J.: Prentice-Hall.

Stocking, M.L., & Lord, F.M. (1983). Developing a common metric in item response theory. *Applied Psychological Measurement*, *7*(2), 201–210.

Ullman, J.D. (1982). *Principles of database systems*. Rockville, Md.: Computer Science Press.

Toward the Development
of Expert Assessment Systems

Ted S. Hasselbring

George Peabody College of Vanderbilt University

ABSTRACT. Artificially intelligent (AI) computer programs are emerging in several disciplines including education. This paper provides an overview of one type of AI program called, ''expert systems.'' The potential application of expert systems to the diagnosis and assessment of special-needs children is examined and existing prototype systems are reviewed. The future of this technology is discussed in relation to emerging development tools designed for the creation of expert systems by the lay public.

The accurate assessment of special-needs children is a critical responsibility for special educators since decisions resulting from assessment can affect a child throughout his or her life. The assessment of special-needs children is a complex, multifaceted process. Salvia and Ysseldyke (1981) define assessment as '' . . . the process of understanding the performance of students in their current ecology'' (p. 4). An accurate and thorough assessment provides educators with the necessary information for making sound instructional programming decisions. Unfortunately, as pointed out by Bennett (1983), some of the most basic tenets of the assessment process are being violated. As a result, there is a long history of poorly conducted assessments and inaccurate interpretations that have led to restricted educational opportunities and inappropriate instructional programs for many special-needs children. Although these incidents have not occurred as the result of malicious intent, they have in no way been in the best interest of handicapped children.

Bennett (1983) suggests several reasons for the inadequate assessment of special-needs children. To begin, the assessment of

Requests for reprints should be sent to: Ted S. Hasselbring, Department of Special Education, George Peabody College, Vanderbilt University, Nashville, TN 37203.

43

special-needs students is a labor-intensive process requiring a significant amount of time and effort. Most special teachers do not have the time required to conduct thorough on-going assessments of their pupils. Second, when teachers do have the time to assess their students, they often do not have the expertise required for selecting the most appropriate evaluation tool. Often, teachers choose diagnostic instruments that are technically inadequate or inappropriate for the purposes of assessment. Third, many teachers do not have the necessary expertise for analyzing evaluation results and developing appropriate intervention programs. The end result is a large number of students that do not receive services and instructional programs meeting their specific needs.

One solution, although practically and economically untenable, would be to have each special-needs child assessed by an expert diagnostician. The full-time responsibility of these diagnosticians would be to provide an on-going assessment of each special-needs child and develop an appropriate remediation program that could be implemented by the child's teacher. Of course, this is unrealistic since there are far too few expert diagnosticians to meet this need. Even if they did exist, schools could not afford to provide such an expensive service.

Another possible solution to this problem is to have the computer act as an assessment and diagnostic expert. To a limited extent this is being done already. Unfortunately, few of the current computer-based assessment programs are capable of functioning at the level of a human expert. For example, computers are being used for scoring and interpreting standardized tests such as the WISC-R, WAIS-R, PIAT, Stanford-Binet, and the Woodcock-Johnson Psycho-Educational Battery. Generally, these tests are given in the traditional manner and the examiner enters the results into the computer. The computer then summarizes and prints out the results in report form. Other computer-based assessment programs perform more of the examiner's functions. In these programs the assessment instrument has actually been encoded into the computer software and the computer is responsible for conducting the assessment, scoring, and summarizing the results. Although these programs alleviate some of the problems associated with the assessment of special-needs students, they can in no way replace the expert diagnostician (Hasselbring, 1984).

There is, however, a relatively new and promising development in computer-based assessment where programs use the principles of artificial intelligence and emulate a human expert. These computer programs, called *expert systems*, are capable of reaching a level of performance comparable to that of a human expert in some specialized problem domain (Nau, 1983). The remainder of this paper will provide an overview of expert systems and describe the potential these programs have for alleviating many of the current problems educators face in assessing special-needs children. In addition, the paper will describe the current state-of-the-art in expert assessment systems and discuss the future of these intelligent programs in student assessment.

OVERVIEW OF EXPERT SYSTEMS

Expert systems, also known as *knowledge-based systems*, have evolved from the field of artificial intelligence over the past 15 years. Hayes-Roth, Waterman, and Lenat (1983) have defined expert systems as automated consulting systems designed to provide the user with expert advice within a particular subject area. These systems embody the knowledge of a particular application area combined with inference mechanisms which enable the program to employ its knowledge in problem-solving situations. Expert systems are unlike conventional computer programs in that they are the first systems designed to help humans solve complex problems in a commonsense way. These systems use the methods and information acquired and developed by a human expert to solve problems, make predictions, suggest possible treatments, and offer advice that is as accurate as its human counterpart.

Ideally, when placed in the same situation, an expert system should provide the user with identical reasoning and play the same role as a human expert. For example, an expert system for diagnosing blood infections might assist an intern in making a diagnosis by asking relevant questions about the suspected infection in the same way a renowned physician would. The intern would respond by answering these questions and would continue this dialogue with the computer until the expert system had sufficient data on which to make a diagnosis. Thus, the expert system would function just as a human expert in diagnosing the problem.

Expert systems are by no means restricted to a limited array of problems. Intelligent programs that emulate a human expert have been designed for several different applications. For example,

DENDRAL is an expert system used for determining the chemical structure of unknown compounds through the analysis of experimental data (Buchanan & Feigenbaum, 1978; Feigenbaum, Buchanan, & Lederberg, 1971). MACSYMA, a mathematically oriented expert system, is used by mathematical researchers and physicists for simplifying complex mathematical expressions (Martin & Fateman, 1971). CADUCEUS (Pople, Myers, & Miller, 1975; Pople, 1981) and MYCIN (Shortliffe, 1976) are both used for medical diagnosis. CADUCEUS provides diagnoses in the area of internal medicine and MYCIN gives consultative advice on the diagnosis and therapy of infectious disease. PROSPECTOR is used to assist geologists in mineral exploration and was recently responsible for locating a $100,000,000 deposit of molybdenum (Gashnig, 1979). R1 is an expert system used for configuring DEC/VAX computer systems to customer specifications. R1 has been evaluated and found to be much faster and more accurate than its human counterpart (McDermott, 1981). These examples represent only a few of the better known expert systems in use today. It is believed that about 500 expert systems are now being used on a daily basis in the fields of medicine, science, business, and industry.

With all expert systems the fundamental assumption is that "Knowledge is Power." Specific knowledge of a task is coupled with general problem-solving knowledge to provide expert-level analyses of difficult situations. In order to do this, a substantial amount of information concerning the techniques and procedures employed within the given domain is encoded into the computer software. Contemporary expert systems represent knowledge in one of three ways: rule-based systems, frame-based systems, and blackboard systems. For the sake of simplicity, we will focus our discussion on the commonly used rule-based systems.

Rule-Based Expert Systems

As suggested by Ham (1984), an expert's skill depends largely on the rules he or she derives from knowledge and experience. A human expert often perceives subtle connections among apparently disparate observations that lead to verifiable scientific fact. To the outsider, the human expert appears to rely on intuition or hunches. This intuitive knowledge, though not easily quantified, can be imparted to the computer in the form of rules. Building an expert system means finding an efficient way to represent these rules.

Generally, rules represent a "chunk" of knowledge about a particular field. Most rule-based expert systems contain hundreds of rules which become connected to each other to form rule networks. Rules represent the facts, beliefs, and heuristics or "rules of thumb," that an expert uses in solving a specific problem. These rules are used by the program to produce an internal representation that makes it an expert about a specific class of problem. The program itself is only an interpreter and a general-reasoning mechanism. This illustrates an important distinction between rule-based expert systems and more conventional computer programs. As shown in Figure 1, in a rule-based system there is a clear separation between the general knowledge about the problem (the rules in the knowledge base), information about a specific problem (facts entered about the current problem), and methods for applying the general knowledge to the problem (the rule interpreter). This partitioning of the rules and facts from the general reasoning mechanism does not occur in traditional computer programs.

System components. Hayes-Roth, Waterman, and Lenat (1983) have represented an idealized expert system as shown in Figure 2. Though no existing expert system contains all of the components

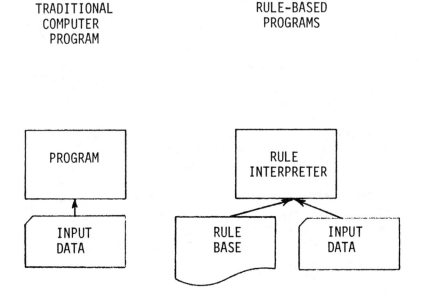

FIGURE 1. Contrast between a traditional program and a rule-based expert system.

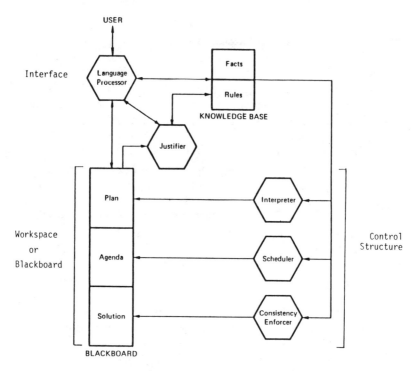

FIGURE 2. Components of an expert system (adapted from Hayes-Roth, Waterman, & Lenat, 1983).

shown, one or more of these components is found in every expert system. To begin, the ideal expert system contains a *language processor* which is able to mediate information exchanges between the user and the expert system. Usually some restricted form of English is used. The language processor interprets the user's questions, commands, and other information. Also, the system should be able to provide answers to questions and explanations for its behavior.

The *knowledge base* consists of two parts, rules which represent the human expert's knowledge about how to solve a problem, and facts which are concerned with the specific problem in question. Facts are often represented in the form, "The <attribute> of <object> is <value> with <certainty>." An example is, "The type of infection is bacterial (.6)."

Rules are most often found in the form, "if A, then B," where A is a single fact or the combination of several facts, and B is another fact. For example, the following if-then rule comes from the MYCIN system used to perform medical diagnosis:

IF: (1) The site of the culture is blood, and
　　(2) The identity of the organism is not known with certainty, and
　　(3) The stain of the organism is gram negative, and
　　(4) The morphology of the organism is rod, and
　　(5) The patient has been seriously burned
THEN: There is weakly suggestive evidence (.4) that the identity of the organism is pseudomonas.

This example illustrates the basic representation of facts and rules within a rule-based expert system.

A third component of an ideal expert system is a *blackboard* which serves as an intermediate workspace for recording the system's hypotheses and decisions. Figure 2 shows three types of decisions recorded on the blackboard, these include: plan, agenda, and solution elements. Plan elements describe the overall plan of attack the system will use to solve the current problem. The agenda elements record the potential actions or rules that are awaiting execution. The solution elements represent the hypotheses and decisions generated thus far that constitute possible solutions to the problem, as well as how these solutions are related to each other.

The *control structure* uses the intermediate decisions from the blackboard, as well as information from the knowledge base to determine the order of the entire problem-solving process. The control structure is generally made up of three components: the interpreter, scheduler, and consistency enforcer. The scheduler is responsible for determining which rule is to be executed next, while the interpreter carries out the task. The consistency enforcer attempts to maintain a consistent representation of the emerging solution. The idea is to ensure that plausible conclusions are obtained and inconsistent ones are rejected.

The remaining component of an ideal expert system is the *justifier*. The justifier is responsible for explaining the actions of the system to the user. An expert system should be able to answer questions posited by the user as to why certain conclusions were reached and others rejected.

THE STATUS OF EXPERT ASSESSMENT SYSTEMS IN EDUCATION

Current expert systems technology seems best suited to diagnosis or classification problems whose solutions depend primarily on the possession of a large amount of specialized, factual, and empirical knowledge (Duda & Shortliffe, 1983). Thus, it is only logical that expert systems be developed in education for assessing learning and behavior problems. Currently, several prototype expert systems are being developed to assist in the assessment of special-needs children.

Reading Assessment

Colbourn and McLeod (1983) have developed a prototype expert system that assists teachers in the assessment of reading problems. The system guides the user through reading diagnosis from the initial suspicion that a reading problem exists to the point at which sufficient information has been gathered to plan an appropriate remedial program. Depending upon available data, the system may request information regarding the student's academic history or suggest that a particular standardized test be administered.

This expert system does not test the student directly, nor does it manage testing activities. Rather, at each step of the diagnosis, the system advises the user as to what data to collect. The teacher or diagnostician performs the suggested task and enters the resulting information into the system. After these new data have been entered, the system analyzes the information and proposes the next step in the assessment process. When a sufficient amount of information has been gathered and entered, the system provides a report of its diagnostic findings. The teacher can then plan a remedial program based upon these results. An obvious extension of this system is to have it prescribe appropriate remedial strategies and instructional techniques based upon the diagnostic findings. The system has been designed to readily include this feature.

With this expert system, as with most others, a dialogue is conducted with the user; the system poses questions or makes suggestions. If the desired information is not available, the system provides the user with the option of stopping the dialogue in order to obtain the necessary information. If this information cannot be obtained, the system continues the diagnostic process, although it often suggests hypotheses with less certainty than if the missing data were available. In cases where critical data are missing, the system reiterates what data are required and then terminates the session.

The performance of this particular expert assessment system has been compared with that of human diagnosticians. When subjected to a number of test cases, the expert system's diagnostic reports were found to be as accurate as those of the human diagnosticians. Further, the reports generated by the system included more information than those of the human diagnosticians and were more consistent in terms of style, content, readability, and accuracy.

Math Assessment

One of the most advanced expert systems for diagnosing student learning problems is DEBUGGY (Burton, 1982). DEBUGGY is designed to diagnose student errors or "bugs" in the domain of place-value subtraction. DEBUGGY is based on the "Buggy Model" (Brown & Burton, 1978) where student errors are seen as symptoms of a "bug." Thus, student errors are not seen as random and DEBUGGY attempts to determine the student's "buggy" rules for solving the problem. DEBUGGY does this by hypothesizing the student's bugs, then attempts to predict not only whether the student will get a similar problem incorrect, but also what the exact answer will be.

DEBUGGY begins the diagnostic process by considering a set of hypotheses which includes 110 primitive bugs and about 20 compound bugs. DEBUGGY is a non-interactive system where the student's answers to a set of subtraction problems (and the problems themselves) are entered into the program by the examiner. DEBUGGY then compares the results of all 130 bugs with the student's answers. This comparison is used to establish an initial set of hypotheses as to the student's problem(s). The initial hypotheses (i.e., bugs that explain at least one incorrect answer) are then combined to generate additional hypotheses about the student. Next the system starts to eliminate hypotheses by finding and removing bugs that are completely subsumed by other primitive bugs. This reduction procedure continues until each of the remaining hypotheses is classified in terms of how well it explains the student's answers. The classification procedure takes into account the number of predicted correct and incorrect answers as well as the number and type of faulty predictions. The goal of the classification procedure is to put each of the hypotheses into one of the four following classes: consistent bug; consistent bug, but with other symptoms; some buggy responses, but not consistent; and unsystematic responses.

An important consideration with DEBUGGY is the set of

problems given the student. The problem set must be able to distinguish all of the primitive and compound bugs. Though this can generally be accomplished with a test containing no more than 20 problems, by tailoring a test to a student based upon initial hypotheses, the effectiveness of the diagnostic procedure can be enhanced. Such an interactive version of DEBUGGY, called IDEBUGGY, has been developed.

IDEBUGGY has the potential for allowing a much faster, better-confirmed diagnosis because the problem sequence can be tailored to the student. IDEBUGGY presents the student with problems and, using the student's responses, generates and maintains a set of possible diagnoses. After each student response, the system decides whether to give another problem or to stop and report the diagnosis. Each new problem is determined by the state of possible diagnoses up to that point. When enough evidence for one hypotheses is collected, and there are no competing hypotheses, the system provides a diagnosis.

Other Prototype Expert Systems

Currently, several other expert assessment systems for use with special-needs children are under development. At Peabody, the author and his colleagues are developing an expert system that assists in assessment and intervention for students with maladaptive social behavior. The system is being developed using a commercially available software tool designed solely for the creation of expert systems. When completed, the system will operate on an IBM Personal Computer and will assist the user in selecting instruments and techniques for assessing inappropriate behaviors. In addition, the system will help the user plan an intervention strategy for extinguishing those behaviors and will assist in evaluating the effectiveness of that plan.

Additional work in expert assessment systems is being conducted at Utah State University by Alan Hofmeister and his colleagues. The expert systems under development at Utah State deal with the assessment and diagnosis of learning disabilities and the assessment of basic math skills. These systems are also being developed using software tools especially designed for the creation of expert systems (Hofmeister, 1985). Development tools such as the ones being used at Peabody and Utah State will be discussed in the following section.

THE FUTURE DEVELOPMENT OF
EXPERT ASSESSMENT SYSTEMS

Probably the greatest single factor affecting the future of expert assessment systems is the growing number of development tools available to the lay public. Generally, these tools are designed so that individuals wishing to develop an expert system can do so without having to program in a complex AI computer language such as LISP or PROLOG. Instead of programming, the developer uses a tool for creating the knowledge and rule bases. The developer need not worry about creating the inference mechanism since this is taken care of by the development tool.

These tools are being made available in increasingly large numbers. At present, several commercially available development tools exist that can be used on today's microcomputers. Some of the available tools include: Expert's Choice, Expert Ease, Exsys, M1, REVEAL, and ES/P Adivsor. (For a detailed review of these development tools see the January 28, 1985 issue of *InfoWorld* or the April 16, 1985 issue of *PC*.) These development tools range in price from $300 to $10,000, and all will operate on a personal computer.

As of now, it is unclear as to whether these tools are sufficiently robust for the development of the type of expert assessment systems that can be used with special-needs children. It is questionable as to whether useful expert assessment systems can be developed within the memory and processing speed constraints imposed by today's personal computers. Within two years, however, information about the utility of these tools will be available: both Peabody and Utah State should have evaluative data on these tools by that time.

Though we are presently limited by hardware and software constraints, the normal pace of progress in these technologies suggests that within a few years hardware and software character-istics will no longer impose a significant barrier. A far greater barrier to future development efforts will be the creation of expert knowledge and rule bases. This process requires that a "human expert" spend months or even years specifying the information, rules, and judgments that are required to make the system function. Few experts have the time to develop these systems. Further, some experts may not want to impart their knowledge to a computer program that may potentially take their place. Thus, the development of these systems will be a very slow process at best.

As with anything new, these development tools have both positive and negative aspects. On the positive side, the creation of expert assessment systems will require developers to learn more about the assessment process itself. As pointed out by Michaelsen, Michie, and Boulanger (1985), "When you build expert systems, you realize that the power behind them is that they provide a regimen for experts to crystallize and codify their knowledge, and in the knowledge lies the power" (p. 311). The process of developing rule and knowledge bases for these systems will force developers to analyze the assessment process more closely than it has ever been analyzed before. There is no doubt that as these systems are developed and evaluated it will become painfully obvious that we do not know as much about assessment and diagnosis as we might think. In effect, the development of expert systems will guide our research and require us to learn more about areas where current understanding is fuzzy. The end result of developing expert assessment systems will be a constant re-examination of the assessment process. This re-examination should in turn lead to a much better understanding of the process and to its eventual improvement.

On the negative side, one must view the emergence of expert systems development tools with mixed emotion. As with any tool, if used with respect and care, benefits can result. On the other hand, if used carelessly, the outcome can be disastrous: the future of expert assessment systems requires that we use development tools cautiously. We must avoid creating a large number of "expert systems" that are pedagogically unsound and potentially dangerous. Even with this caution, it is inevitable that over the next few years there will be a plethora of so called "expert assessment systems," but few will be truly "expert." As with the early CAI software, only a handful of these systems will live up to the claims made for them and many will not be worth the price of the floppy disk they are stored on.

SUMMARY

Though expert systems are relatively new to education, they are attracting an increasing amount of attention. The development of expert systems for assessing and diagnosing the problems of special-needs children shows great promise. Although existing prototype systems appear to be effective in the assessment and diagnosis of reading and math problems, these systems still require the use of computers more powerful and expensive than the desk-top computers now found in schools. Nevertheless, this is only a temporary problem. A greater concern is the development of useful expert assessment systems. Even though development tools are available, experts are going to have to spend hundreds of hours creating and testing these systems. Without this effort, there is little hope that expert systems will improve the assessment and diagnosis of special-needs children.

REFERENCES

Bennett, R.E. (1983). Research and evaluation priorities for special education assessment. *Exceptional Children, 50*(2), 110-117.

Brown, J.S., & Burton, R.R. (1978). Diagnostic models for procedural bugs in basic mathematical skills. *Cognitive Science, 2*, 155–192.

Buchanan, B.G., & Feigenbaum, E.A. (1978). DENDRAL and Meta-DENDRAL: Their application dimension. *Artificial Intelligence, 11*, 5–24.

Burton, R. (1982). Diagnosing bugs in a simple procedural skill. In D. Sleeman & J. Brown (Eds.), *Intelligent tutoring systems* (pp. 157–183). New York: Academic Press.

Colbourn, M.J., & McLeod, J. (1983). Computer-guided educational diagnosis: A prototype expert system. *Journal of Special Education Technology, 6*, 30–39.

Duda, R., & Shortliffe, E. (1983). Expert systems research. *Science, 220*, 261–268.

Feigenbaum, E.A., Buchanan, B.G., & Lederberg, J. (1971). On generality and problem solving: A case study using the DENDRAL program. In B. Meltzer and D. Michie (Eds.), *Machine Intelligence, Vol. 6.* (pp. 165–190). Edinburgh: Edinburgh University Press.

Gashnig, J. (1979). Preliminary performance analysis of the PROSPECTOR consultant system for mineral exploration. *Proceedings of the 6th International Joint Conference on Artificial Intelligence (IJCAI)*, 308–310.

Ham, M. (1984, January). Playing by the rules. *PC World*, pp. 34–41.

Hasselbring, T.S. (1984). Computer-based assessment of special-needs students. In Bennett, R.E., & Maher, C.A. (Eds.), *Microcomputers and Exceptional Children*, New York: The Haworth Press.

Hayes-Roth, F., Waterman, D.A., & Lenat, D.B. (1983). An overview of expert systems. In F. Hayes-Roth, D.A. Waterman, & D.B. Lenat (Eds.), *Building Expert Systems* (pp. 3–30). Reading, MA: Addison-Wesley Publishing Company, Inc.

Hofmeister, A.M. (1985, January). Personal Communication.

Martin, W.A., & Fateman, R. J. (1971). The MACSYMA system. *Proceedings of the Second Symposium on Symbolic and Algebraic Manipulation*, (pp. 59–75). Los Angeles.

McDermott, J. (1981). R1: The formative years. *AI Magazine, 2*, 21–29.

Michaelsen, R.H., Michie, D., & Boulanger, A. (1985). The technology of expert systems. *Byte, 9*, 303–312.

Nau, D. (1983). Expert computer systems. *IEEE Computer 16*, 63–85.

Pople, H.E., Jr. (1981). Heuristic methods for imposing structure on ill-structured problems: The structuring of medical diagnostics. In P. Szolovitz (Ed.), *Artificial Intelligence in Medicine* (pp. 119–185). American Association for the Advancement of Science. Boulder, CO: Westview Press.

Pople, H.E., Jr., Myers, J.D., & Miller, R.A. (1975). DIALOG: A model of diagnostic logic for internal medicine. In *Proceedings of the 4th International Joint Conference on Artificial Intelligence (IJCAI)*, 848–855.

Salvia, J., & Ysseldyke, J.E. (1981). *Assessment in special and remedial education* (2nd ed.). Boston: Houghton Mifflin Company.

Shortliffe, E.H. (1976). *Computer-based medical consultation: MYCIN*. New York: American Elsevier.

Functional Psychoeducational Assessment: Trends and Issues

Daniel J. Reschly

Iowa State University

ABSTRACT. Careful match of assessment process and procedure to the decision(s) to be made is seen as the most important step in improving psychoeducational assessment. Clarification of the decision(s) to be made is best achieved through referral assessment and pre-referral interventions. Trends in assessment, particularly greater use of behavioral approaches and natural settings, are also emphasized.

The emphasis in the title on functional assessment may seem trite to the naive reader. The obvious question is: Do people collect assessment data that is not functional or useful? The answer is, unfortunately, that much of the assessment data routinely collected are not used very well, often because they are not particularly useful for a variety of reasons.

Assessment is defined as gathering information to make decisions (Salvia & Ysseldyke, 1985). This rather broad definition could encompass a wide variety of purposes, approaches, and processes. However, before contemplating all the things that might be included as assessment, it is useful to transpose the concepts in the definition and then contemplate, on what bases should important decisions about students be made? This shifts our initial focus away from assessment approaches or techniques to consideration of decisions that need to be made.

Perhaps the most important single influence on whether useful assessment information is generated is the question of purpose or what decision must be made. If the purpose for assessment is

---

Requests for reprints should be sent to: Daniel J. Reschly, Department of Psychology, Iowa State University, Ames, IA 50011.

defined clearly, then it is possible for assessment information to be generated which is closely related to the purpose or the decision to be made. If the purpose is not defined clearly, then the assessment information may very well reflect customary practices, traditional approaches, or the theoretical orientation of the psychologist, all of which may be quite irrelevant to the decision that must be made. Emphasis on the decision to be made clearly implies that the context in which the information is gathered and used is extremely important. Careful consideration of purpose and context enhances the likelihood of useful assessment, i.e., assessment closely tied to decisions to be made about students.

PURPOSES OF ASSESSMENT

Purposes of assessment are discussed in virtually every textbook on psychological and educational measurement (e.g., Anastasi, 1982; Brown, 1983; Taylor, 1984; Salvia & Ysseldyke, 1985). The assessment carried out by school psychologists and other persons associated with programs for handicapped students most often involves the purposes of classification/placement and/or program planning/intervention. Other purposes, not discussed in this article, are certainly important, e.g., evaluation of program effects for groups (Maher & Bennett, 1984). Due to space limitations, however, only two of the most common purposes of assessment are discussed in this article.

Referral Assessment and Clarification

Individual assessment by special services personnel is initiated most often when a student is referred, usually by the classroom teacher (Bickel, 1982). Teacher referrals most often arise due to problems in achievement, inappropriate social behavior, or both. The referral is often motivated by considerable concern, sometimes frustration, with the behavior and development of a specific student. Sometimes, the referral agent simply wants the student removed from the classroom.

For a variety of reasons, the usual focus of individual assessment is the child, not the teacher, classroom environment, or educational system. Consideration of this broader context is essential to functional assessment. No classroom problem exists in a vacuum, or exclusively within the student. Other variables, from typical behavior of peers to teacher attitudes must be considered if effective solutions are to be developed. Context must be considered during the referral assessment and clarification.

Because the referral is a crucial part of psychoeducational assessment, an essential principle is the necessity to clarify referral concerns and to assess the nature of the referral. Referral clarification and assessment involves several data gathering activities which can be carried out through interview, classroom observation, and review of educational records. Initial referral statements typically are vague and global (e.g., poor achievement or disruptive behavior). These vague, global statements should be clarified and restated in more precise language (e.g., reads below grade level, has poor word attack skills, cannot complete work independently). Previous and current educational programs and teaching methods should be investigated. Prior efforts to resolve the problems should be examined. If considerable effort has not already been devoted to resolving the problem within the regular school program, intervention should be designed, implemented, monitored, and evaluated *prior* to consideration of classifying the student as handicapped. Prereferral interventions are increasingly viewed as essential in policy statements concerning education of mildly handicapped students (Graden, Casey, & Christianson, 1985; Heller, Holtzman, & Messick, 1982).

Several methods have been developed in recent years to clarify and assess referrals (Batsche, 1985; Bergan & Kratochwill, 1985; Tombari, 1981). These methods generally involve interviewing the person who made the referral as well as carefully examining current and previous educational records. This information should lead to a set of precise questions, mutually agreed upon by the teacher and special services personnel, which are then used to guide the individual's comprehensive evaluation. These procedures also help ensure that the referral is appropriate and clearly understood by all persons. Failure to assess the referral and to clarify concerns, often leads to poor communication among the professionals involved, as well as to irrelevant assessment activities. In all too many instances, measures largely irrelevant to referral questions (Keogh, Kukic, Becker, McLaughlin & Kukic, 1975; Ysseldyke, Thurlow, Graden, Wesson, Algozzine, & Deno, 1983) or technically inadequate assessment procedures (Ysseldyke et al., 1983), have been used in both school and clinical settings (Wade and Baker, 1977).

Classification/Placement

Classification/Placement decisions address the following questions of eligibility: (1) Can the student be classified as handicapped? (2) Is the student eligible for chapter I or other special programs? If the student can be classified as handicapped using state or federal rules or regulations, the next question to be answered is whether special education is required. It is important to note that both questions must be answered affirmatively, in the order given (i.e., classification first, then determination of need for placement) before placement in special education can be justified. It is possible, although rare, for a student to meet the criteria as handicapped, but *not* need special education or related services.

Classification/Placement decisions generally involve comparing an individual's pattern of behavior with age or grade level expectations and norms. The kind of assessment needed for classification/placement decisions is often called *norm referenced*, because the individual's performance is compared to typical performance of some group, usually a representative sample of other students of the same age or grade level. The key questions in norm referenced assessment focus on: (1) general areas of concern, (2) level of performance, (3) pattern of performance, and (4) degree of difference in relation to age or grade level expectations. Comparisons are most often made through the use of standardized tests, but other methods have been recently developed including classroom norms for behavior assessment (Alessi & Kaye, 1983) and curriculum based assessment (Ysseldyke et al. 1983).

Criteria to evaluate norm referenced assessment procedures are available in a variety of standard texts, several of which were cited earlier. Briefly, these criteria require that: (1) the test items or observation events must reflect the behavior of concern (content validity), (2) the behavior of concern must be representative of a developmentally important domain of behavior, (3) the items or observations must be sufficiently reliable to infer level of competence, (4) a representative sample to develop stable norms be available, (5) appropriate derived scores be available, (6) subtests or composite scores used for classification purposes be highly reliable, and (7) comparisons of scores reflecting different domains of behavior (e.g., ability and achievement) be on the same score scale. Several examples of assessment personnel failing to consider these basic criteria have been reported in recent years (Bennett & Shepherd, 1982; Shepard 1983).

Program Planning/Intervention

Program planning/intervention involves decisions about what needs to be learned or treated. Precise information on specific skills or competencies is needed. In contrast to classification/placement, there is little need for comparison to other students. The decisions here deal with what to teach or to treat, what methods or strategies to use, and how to evaluate instructional or intervention effectiveness.

Assessment to address these questions is typically criterion referenced; it is designed to pinpoint as precisely as possible what students can and cannot do in some important domain of behavior. The general guidelines for sound criterion referenced assessment require: (1) items or observations clearly related to important objectives, (2) *thorough* assessment of each objective, and (3) objectives organized into a meaningful hierarchy or developmental sequence.

It is perhaps important to note that most currently available instruments standardized or informal, do not meet the criteria for *both* norm referenced and criterion-referenced assessment. Most instruments are useful for one or the other purpose.

Purpose-Assessment Procedures Match

Perhaps the most crucial decision, requiring the highest level of skill, is insuring a close match between referral questions, purposes for assessment and assessment procedures. The decisions contemplated are crucial to the educational careers of students and ultimately to their adult lives. A close match is far more likely to lead to appropriate classification/placement decisions and effective interventions. A poor match can generate information that is relatively useless for either purpose. Many of the assessment trends described in the following section reflect efforts to insure a much closer match between assessment and decision-making.

TRENDS IN ASSESSMENT

There are several trends in current assessment theory, research, and practice which can enhance generation of functional data. Many of these trends, although stemming from diverse influences, have the same general effect: generation of assessment data useful for decision-making. The nature of these trends is similar in that they are more consistent with behavioral approaches to the analysis of learning and behavior problems.

Links Between Assessment, Intervention, and Evaluation

A major continuing problem in special education is demonstrating the positive effects of these programs. As resources become increasingly scarce, pressure to demonstrate positive benefits can be expected to intensify. The overall effect is to place greater emphasis on the evaluation of program outcomes and to foster further development of assessment technology which can be useful in the evaluation of those outcomes.

A variety of methods have been described for evaluation of programs (Maher & Bennett, 1984). A very important trend in this area is the increased use of assessment systems to provide continuous data throughout the identification, intervention, and evaluation process (see Deno, Marston & Tindal, this volume). These data are used to identify important target behaviors, to establish objectives for instruction or treatment, to monitor progress of instruction or treatment as the basis for modifications in programs, and finally, to evaluate effects. These continuous measurement systems enhance the value of assessment by providing information useful for making decisions at all stages of the intervention process.

Natural Settings

The second major trend is increased emphasis upon assessment in natural settings where children and adults live, play, and work. Collection of assessment data in the natural setting greatly enhances consideration of context variables and the likelihood that the information derived will be relevant to the identification and amelioration of problems. The natural settings used can include the classroom, playground, home, or neighborhood. The trend is toward collecting behavioral samples from the natural setting rather than entirely relying on standardized test items to sample important domains of behavior (Deno, Mirken, & Chiang, 1982; Ysseldyke et al., 1983). These authors have described methods whereby reading samples are selected from the classroom basal reading series and then used to assess the youngster's skill level in reading. These samples are apparently quite accurate in identifying students who are markedly below average classroom performance. Many other such examples of assessment in natural settings exist. The primary point is increased use of samples of behavior drawn from existing, ongoing activities in the natural setting. Similar developments, although not well refined to date, are also apparent in the assessment of social/emotional behaviors (Gresham, 1985; Gresham & Elliott, 1984).

Behavioral Assessment

Behavioral assessment continues to expand in breadth and sophistication of technology. Anyone who dismissed behavioral assessment some years ago as being excessively narrow or too restrictive is strongly encouraged to look at some of the recent literature in this field (e.g., Kratochwill, 1982). Behavioral assessment procedures now reflect broad classes of behavior such as cognitive style, social skills, anxiety, and so forth. The behavioral assessment techniques have been refined to include a variety of instruments and observation methods. Some of the different methods not only include observation methods, but also structured interviews (Gresham & Elliott, 1984), rating scales (Edelbrock, 1983), and various self-report procedures.

It is important to note that these procedures are not assumed a priori to be reliable and valid, but must be consistent with other indices reflecting the target behavior. This use of multiple sources of information gathered from the same behavioral domain provides an appropriate means of protecting against the lower reliability of single instruments or assessment procedures. For example, peer relations are arguably a crucial feature of effective programming for handicapped students (Gresham, 1985; Reschly, Gresham, & Graham-Clay, 1984). None of the currently available peer relations measures has sufficient reliability to be used in making a decision about an individual student if stringent criteria, such as those proposed by Salvia & Ysseldyke (1985), are applied. However, a number of methods of assessing peer relations are available, such as teacher interview, observation, sociometrics, and various checklists. If the results from several measures are consistent, the observation about peer relations is reliable and can be a very useful addition to educational programming.

Lower Level of Inference

Level of inference refers to the relationship between the behavior observed and the meaning attributed to that behavior. There is a long and unfortunate tradition in applied areas of psychology of highly inferential interpretations of rather simple behavioral events. A classic clinical text by Rapaport, Gill, & Shafer (1968) provides an entire volume devoted, for the most part, to highly inferential interpretations using traditional psychological tests like figure copying, intellectual assessment, and projective devices. The Bender Motor Gestalt Test (Bender, 1938) is one of the most frequently used psychological tests with children and adults. The Bender, which involves a series of 8 relatively simple geometric designs which the individual is to copy, is used in this article as an example of an assessment device which can be interpreted using different levels of inference. Other devices including intelligence tests such as the Wechsler scales could also have been used as examples. The point being made has to do with the relationship between behavior observed and the meaning attributed to that behavior; a general point relevant to a wide variety of assessment procedures, not just the Bender.

In Figure 1, two reproductions of one of the Bender items are provided. The very poor drawing noted as Danny's Bender might be interpreted, depending on theoretical orientation of the psychologist, as revealing poor copying skills or poor visual-motor skills. Both of these interpretations reflect a relatively low level of inference since there is a fairly close relationship between the meaning attributed to the behavior and the behavior actually observed. The higher level of inference would be reflected in an interpretation indicating immaturity or developmental lag; a very common type of interpretation of poor Bender drawings. Considerably higher levels of inference are reflected in interpretations of poor Bender drawings which propose neurological dysfunction, possible hemispheric specialization, or emotional/personality status. In much of the very traditional clinical literature, the drawing which appears in the figure is believed to reveal personality conflicts having to do with sexual relationships. An obvious question is to what extent does the very simple behavioral event of attempting to reproduce the Bender design have to do with deep, underlying personality dynamics or hemispherisity?

Highly inferential interpretations, of the Bender or other devices,

Figure 1

Different Levels of Inference In

Interpretation of Bender Reproductions

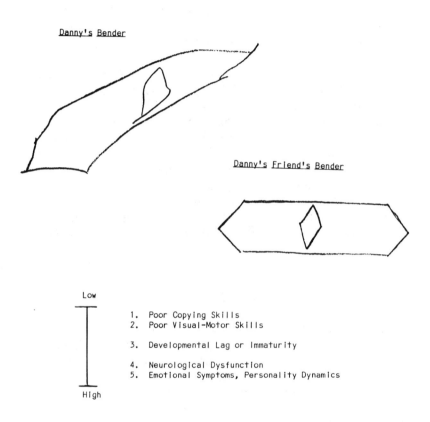

Danny's Bender

Danny's Friend's Bender

Low

1. Poor Copying Skills
2. Poor Visual-Motor Skills

3. Developmental Lag or Immaturity

4. Neurological Dysfunction
5. Emotional Symptoms, Personality Dynamics

High

are generally not functional for a variety of reasons. First, these interpretations are rarely supported by research data. Perhaps the best known source for Bender interpretation with children (Koppitz, 1975), includes a number of cautions concerning the empirical basis for highly inferential interpretations, but later in the same source, such interpretations are presented rather unequivocally. For persons deeply committed to these kinds of interpretations, (e.g., especially use of the Bender emotional indicators) careful *reading* of the references cited by Koppitz is quite instructive. In fact, the empirical basis for most of the highly inferential interpretations of the Bender is virtually nonexistent. The empirical basis for other highly inferential interpretations, particularly those which suggest underlying personality dynamics, is similarly almost always without empirical foundation.

A second problem with highly inferential interpretation is that the variables identified (e.g., repressed hostility) are usually very difficult, if not impossible, to influence through instruction or treatment. Third, highly inferential interpretations are rarely related to educational interventions or psychological treatments (i.e., treatment method is not improved through knowledge of highly inferential interpretations). Finally, highly inferential interpretations, because they focus on deep underlying problems, frequently deflect interest from treatment or intervention. Problems described in terms of neurological dysfunction or deep underlying emotional conflict certainly do not seem to be directly amenable to instruction or treatment. On the other hand, straightforward, precise descriptions of the same behaviors without the presumed underlying causes or dynamics are much more likely to be regarded as amenable to instruction or treatment (Bergan and Kratochwill, 1985; Tombari & Bergan, 1978).

CONCLUSIONS

Increased emphasis on functional assessment is one of the most potentially beneficial trends in human services today. By definition, functional assessment concerns decision-making and efforts to enhance intervention effectiveness. As noted earlier, there are a variety of influences which are stimulating greater concern for more functional assessment. A major influence is legal activity in the form of legislation and litigation (Bersoff, 1982; Reschly, 1983, in press). Federal legislation and litigation have fostered far greater attention to the use of assessment data in designing interventions. These legal influences are expected to provide increasingly strong impetus for highly desirable changes in the assessment services provided by professionals.

Another major influence toward more functional assessment is the effort to reform the existing exceptional child classification system. Although this enormously complicated issue is beyond the scope of this article, it is important to note that the major trends discussed in this article reflect key elements of proposals to reform this system (Reynolds & Wang, 1983; Wang & Birch, 1984). A final major influence toward more functional assessment is the continuing concern for nondiscrimination in placement and fairness in educational programming for disadvantaged, or minority students. The major underlying issue in the placement bias litigation which, unfortunately, was largely ignored by the courts, was effectiveness of special education programs (Heller, Holtzman & Messick, 1982; Reschly, 1981, 1984). If the tests used for educational placement decisions could have been demonstrated to be functionally related to rational classification decisions and effective instructional programs, it is highly likely that certain cases (*Larry P.*, 1979, 1984; *Marshall*, 1984; *PASE*, 1980) would never have been brought to the courts.

A variety of movements are associated with efforts to enhance the usefulness of assessment. These diverse influences all seem to point to the need for assessment data which is functional in the sense of being clearly related to educational programming decisions, and useful in the sense of producing effective interventions. Not all assessment data are functional, and seemingly sophisticated techniques applied by highly trained individuals often lead to useless results. The keys to functional assessment are clear specification of purposes, rigorous matching of assessment process and procedures to referral questions, and application of assessment technologies designed to enhance decision making and effective programming.

REFERENCES

Alessi, G. & Kaye, J. (1983). *Behavioral Assessment for School Psychologists.* Washington, D.C.: National Association of School Psychologists.
Anastasi, A. (1982). *Psychological testing (5th Ed.).* New York: MacMillan.
Batsche, G. (1985). *Referral Oriented Case Consultation.* Washington, D.C.: National Association of School Psychologists.
Bender, L.A. (1938). A Visual Motor Gestalt Test and its Clinical Use. *Research Monographs of the American Psychiatric Association,* No. 3.
Bennett, R.E. & Shepherd, M.J. (1982). Basic measurement proficiency of learning disability specialists. *Learning Disability Quarterly, 5,* 177–184.
Bergan, J. & Kratochwill, T. (1985). *Behavioral consultation.* New York: Plenum.
Bersoff, D.N. (1982a). The legal regulation of school psychology. In C.R. Reynolds & T.B. Gutkin (Eds.). *The Handbook of School Psychology.* New York: John Wiley.
Brown, F.G. (1983). *Principles of educational and psychological testing* (3rd Ed.). New York: Holt, Rinehart, & Winston.
Bickel, W.E. (1982). Classifying mentally retarded students: A review of placement practices in special education. In K.A. Heller, W.H. Holtzman, & S. Messick (Eds.). *Placing*

Children in Special Education: A Strategy for Equity. Washington, D.C.: National Academy Press.

Deno, S.L., Mirkin, P.K., & Chiang, B. (1982). Identifying valid measures of reading. *Exceptional Children, 49*, 36–45.

Edelbrock, C. (1983). Problems and issues in using rating scales to assess child personality and child psychopathology. *School Psychology Review, 12*, 293–299.

Graden, J.L., Casey, A., & Christianson, S.L. (1985). Implementing a prereferral intervention system: Part I. The model. *Exceptional Children, 51*, 377–384.

Gresham, F.M. (1985). Social skills. In A. Thomas & J. Grimes (Eds.), *Best Practices in School Psychology*. Kent, OH: National Association of School Psychologists.

Gresham, F.M. & Elliott, S.N. (1984). Assessment and classification of children's social skills: A review of methods and issues. *School Psychology Review, 13*, 242–301.

Heller, K., Holtzman, W. & Messick, S. (Eds.) (1982). *Placing Children in Special Education: A Strategy for Equity*. Washington, D.C.: National Academy Press.

Keogh, B., Kukic, S., Becker, L., McLaughlin, R., & Kukic, M. (1975). School psychologists' services in special education programs. *Journal of School Psychology, 13*, 142–148.

Koppitz, E. (1975). *The Bender Gestalt Test for Young Children (Vol. 2): Research and . Application, 1963–1973*. New York: Grune & Stratton.

Kratochwill, T.R. (1982). Advances in behavioral assessment. In C.R. Reynolds & T.B. Gutkin. *The Handbook of School Psychology*. New York: Wiley.

Larry P. v. Riles, 343 F. Supp. 1306 (N. D. Cal. 1972) (preliminary injunction). Aff'd 502 F. 2d 963 (9th Cir. 1974); 495 F. Sup. 926 (N. D. Cal. 1979) (decision on merits) aff'd (9th Cir. No. 80-427 Jan. 23, 1984).

Maher, C., & Bennett, R. (1984). *Planning and evaluating special education services*. Englewood Cliffs, N.J.: Prentice-Hall.

Marshall et al. v. Georgia. U.S. District Court for the Southern District of Georgia, CV 482-233, June 28, 1984.

PASE (Parents in Action on Special Education vs. Joseph P. Hannon. U.S. District Court, Northern District of Illinois, Eastern Division, No. 74 (3578), July, 1980.

Rapaport, D., Gill, M., & Schafer, R. (1968). *Diagnostic psychological testing* (Rev. ed. by R. Holt). New York: International Universities Press.

Reschly, D. (1981). Psychological testing in educational classification and placement. *American Psychologist, 36*, 1094–1102. (a)

Reschly, D. (1983). Legal issues in psychoeducational assessment. In G. Hynd (Ed.). *The school psychologist: Contemporary perspectives*. Syracuse, N.Y.: Syracuse University Press.

Reschly, D.J. (1984). Beyond IQ test bias: The national academy panel's analysis of minority EMR overrepresentation. *Educational Researcher, 13(3)*, 15–19.

Reschly, D. (in press). Assessing educational handicaps. In A. Hess & I. Weiner (Eds.). *Handbook of Forensic Psychology*. New York: Wiley.

Reschly, D.J., Gresham, F.M., & Graham-Clay, S. *Multi-factored Nonbiased Assessment: Convergent and Discriminant Validity of Social and Cognitive Measures with Black and White Regular and Special Education Students*. Final Project Report. Department of Psychology, Iowa State University, Ames, IA 50011. ERIC ED NO.

Reynolds, M.C. & Wang, M. (1983). Restructuring "special" school programs: A position paper. *Policy Studies Review, 2* (Special No. 1), 189–212.

Salvia, J. & Ysseldyke, J. (1985). *Assessment in special and remedial education* (3rd Ed.). Boston: Houghton-Mifflin.

Shepard, L.A. (1983). The role of measurement in educational policy: Lessons from the identification of learning disabilities. *Educational Measurement: Issues and Practice, 2*, 4–8.

Taylor, R.L. (1984). *Assessment of Exceptional Students: Educational and Psychological Procedures*. Englewood Cliffs, N.J.: Prentice-Hall.

Tombari, M. (1981). Nonbiased assessment of emotionally disturbed students. In T. Oakland (Ed.) *Nonbiased Assessment*. Minneapolis, MN: National School Psychology Inservice Training Network, University of Minnesota.

Tombari, M. & Bergan, J. (1978). Consultant cues, teacher and teacher verbalizations, judgments, and expectancies for children's adjustment problems. *Journal of School Psychology*, *16*, 212–219.

Wade, T.C. & Baker, T.B. (1977). Opinions and use of psychological tests: A survey of clinical psychologists. *American Psychologist*, *32*, 874–882.

Wang, M.C. & Birch, J.W. (1984). Comparison of a full-time mainstreaming program and a resource room approach. *Exceptional Children*, *51*, 33–40.

Ysseldyke, J.E., Thurlow, M., Graden, J., Wesson, C., Algozzine, B., & Deno, S. (1983). Generalizations from five years of research on assessment and decision making: The University of Minnesota Institute. *Exceptional Education Quarterly*, *4*, 75–93.

Cognitive Assessment
With Disabled Readers

Louise C. Spear

Yale University and Southern Connecticut State University

Robert J. Sternberg

Yale University

ABSTRACT. This paper describes an approach to cognitive assessment that involves a synthesis of the traditional psychometric approach and the more recent information-processing approaches. In this combined approach, psychometric tests are supplemented by tasks adapted from information-processing research. The paper focuses on the use of the approach with disabled readers, although the approach may be generalized to many different populations. The Test of Syllable and Phoneme Counting, a measure of awareness of the sound structure of speech, is described, as an example of an information-processing task that would be useful with younger disabled readers. Guidelines for using information-processing measures are also discussed.

For good or ill, assessment commands much of the time and energy of school personnel. Most of these professionals—special educators, speech and language pathologists, school psychologists, and classroom teachers, among others—would recognize the utility of assessment. However, most of them would also recognize a number of significant problems related to assessment and placement practices.

First, the use of assessment for placing children into currently-used diagnostic categories is fraught with hazard. For example, "emotional disturbance" and "learning disabilities" are diagnoses that connote drastically different behavioral patterns and treatments. In fact, however, such children may exhibit remarkably similar characteristics in the classroom. In addition, the current diagnostic

---

Requests for reprints should be sent to: Robert J. Sternberg, Department of Psychology, Yale University, Box 11A Yale Station, New Haven, CT 06520.

labels engender negative expectations that may detrimentally affect the performance of both students and teachers (Goffman, 1963). Some researchers argue that the negative effects of labeling have been exaggerated (e.g., MacMillan, Jones, & Aloia, 1974). However, there seems to be general agreement that labeling should be avoided unless the label implies a distinctive treatment (Ingalls, 1978), and this is not true of most labels currently used in special education.

Second, although, ideally, the information gained from assessment should be used to improve instruction, the relationship between assessment and teaching is often unclear. Many popularly used tests have content that bears an uncertain or even negligible relationship to what is taught in the classroom. Even when there is an obvious relationship, as in the case of most achievement tests, the tests may be so global that they do not yield helpful information about specific academic difficulties.

Finally, at times, there is a notable lack of communication among the various professional groups involved in assessment. Each professional group tends to have its own terminology, its own underlying philosophy, and its own set of assessment procedures. These differences may foster rivalry and misunderstanding, rather than cooperation, among professionals.

One can identify many types of assessment technique, ranging from formal standardized test batteries to informal checklists and quizzes. In our opening paragraphs, we have focused on more formal assessment devices, the kind exemplifed by tests such as the Wechsler Intelligence Scale for Children, the Stanford-Binet, the Wide Range Achievement Test, and the Peabody Picture Vocabulary Test. These kinds of tests can be identified with the psychometric tradition in psychology, However, in recent years, another line of work in psychology, one which is often contrasted with the psychometric tradition, has gained popularity. This is the cognitive-processing or information-processing approach.

As the name suggests, in the information-processing approach, the emphasis is on process more than on product—on how learning takes place. One example of a research technique employed by information-processing psychologists involves the use of computer simulations. For instance, a psychologist interested in reading comprehension might try to design a computer program that "reads" stories and answers questions about them. The specificity required to design such a computer program, and the logic required to make it work, can provide insights about the kinds of processes involved in reading.

Whereas the psychometric approach has had more to say than the information-processing approach about the structure of human intelligence, the information-processing approach has had more to offer in illuminating the mental processes people use. In many ways, the two approaches can be seen as complementary. We would like to suggest a synthesis of the two, rather than an abandonment of one or the other, as each approach has its strengths and weaknesses. For instance, federal and state guidelines for qualifying handicapped children for special services are tied to the psychometric tradition. Despite the pitfalls of many psychometric tests, such as IQ tests, these measures do provide some degree of objectivity for those engaged in making decisions about which children should receive special services. In addition, until recently, the psychometric approach has had more to say about individual differences in learning than has the information-processing approach.

There is always a trade-off between the amount of time spent on assessment and the usefulness of the information gained from it. Before advocating more assessment, therefore, one must be sure that the knowledge gained will justify the time consumed by testing. However, we believe that, properly used, the information-processing approach does have something important to add to assessment. Most significantly, it can provide the examiner with knowledge about process—about how the child learns. This is the kind of knowledge that is especially relevant to teaching. In addition, this approach tends to avoid the dangers of labeling, less for intrinsic reasons than for historical ones. Because, in the past, information-processing psychologists have not focused on individual differences in learning, the approach has not tended to be used to categorize or label individuals.

In this paper, we will describe our approach to cognitive assessment—that is, assessment techniques derived from information-processing research. We focus on the use of cognitive assessment with disabled readers. By "disabled readers," we refer to individuals who have a severe discrepancy between overall intellectual ability and reading skill, and whose poor reading is not attributable to handicapping conditions other than reading disability, such as hearing impairment or emotional disturbance. We recognize that reading disability is not necessarily limited to individuals of average or above-average intelligence. However, we exclude for now the consideration of disabled readers who are also below average intellectually because it is very difficult to disentangle factors related to the reading disability from those related to general low intelligence.

We emphasize cognitive assessment with disabled readers because our most recent work has involved disabled readers, and because reading disability is one of the most common problems faced by handicapped learners. However, we hasten to add that the general approach described here is applicable to a wide range of exceptionalities, as well as to individuals who are not handicapped.

AN INFORMATION-PROCESSING APPROACH TO READING DISABILITY

We will begin our discussion of an information-processing approach to reading disability with examples of some different types of mental processes (see Sternberg, 1977, for a more detailed discussion). For instance, *learning* processes are employed in acquiring a new skill, *performance* processes are used in carrying out a task, and higher-level *planning* processes are used in decision-making and management of mental resources. Deciding on a strategy for performing a task, and deciding how much time to spend on a task, are examples of higher-level planning processes. The various types of processes are usually measured by analyzing performance on a well-defined task, such as solving pictorial analogies or decoding words. The actual tasks used in the information-processing approach often look quite similar to portions of standard psychometric tests, although the information-processing tasks tend to sample a more specific, narrower domain. The major feature that distinguishes the information-processing approach from the psychometric approach is not the nature of the tasks used. Rather, it is the emphasis on analyzing performance on a task, or a set of related tasks.

We would argue that reading disability involves malfunctioning of learning processes and performance processes related to lower-level skills in reading, such as word decoding. Disorders in higher-level planning processes do not appear to play a central role in reading disability. We base our argument on the most consistent patterns of results in the research literature, and on our own research results (Spear & Sternberg, in press). In the next section, we discuss cognitive assessment techniques stemming from information-processing research with disabled readers.

COGNITIVE ASSESSMENT WITH DISABLED READERS

For the past two years, we have been conducting research designed first to formulate, and later to test, a theoretical framework for understanding reading disability. This line of work provides an example of a synthesis of the psychometric and information-processing approaches to assessment. In this section, we will first present a brief description of the framework. Next, we will discuss some of the test materials, including information-processing kinds of tasks, used in research involving the framework. Finally, we will discuss the implications of the research for the cognitive assessment of disabled readers.

A Theoretical Framework

According to the framework, there are two phases in the progression of a reading disability. The earlier phase involves disabled readers who are nonreaders or at a beginning grade level in reading (i.e., first or second grade). In this phase, the disability manifests itself in a cluster of lower-level problems: difficulty learning to decode individual words, lack of awareness of the sound structure of speech, and deficient use of a speech-based code in short-term memory. Awareness of the sound structure of speech, or phonemic and syllabic awareness, involves the ability to count sounds and syllables in spoken words (e.g., the word "fish" consists of three sounds and one syllable), or to manipulate the sounds in spoken words, as in Pig Latin. A speech-based code in short-term memory appears to be important in proficient reading, in that good readers seem to make use of this kind of code, even during silent reading, to temporarily retain groups of words in short-term memory for later processing (see Crowder, 1982, for further discussion). Both of these deficit areas—lack of awareness of the sound structure of speech, and deficient use of a speech-based code in short-term memory—are precursors of the word-decoding deficit (e.g., Helfgott, 1976; Mann & Liberman, 1982). Due to the heterogeneous nature of the reading disabled population, it is assumed that other, as yet undiscovered, precursors of the disorder exist.

The later phase of the framework involves disabled readers who are reading at a third to fourth grade level or higher. In this phase of the disability, higher-level kinds of difficulties, particularly with reading comprehension and the use of reading and memory strategies, become paramount. However, a central tenet of the framework is that these higher-level difficulties are not attributable to a higher-level processing deficit. Instead, they are attributable to at least three other possible factors. The first factor involves the original constellation of lower-level deficits, which may affect higher-level processing and limit the child's ability to profit from classroom experiences. The second factor consists of the difficulty encountered by disabled readers in automatizing decoding. Even when they can decode accurately, these children seem to decode slowly and only with great effort. Their need to concentrate on decoding thus consumes mental resources that, in good readers, are free for higher-level skills such as comprehension. The third factor is experiential. Disabled readers do not read as much as good readers do, nor do they experience the same academic demands. Lack of experience or practice may exacerbate their problems, especially in the case of older disabled readers, who have a longer history of poor reading.

The importance of the two phases to the assessment of disabled readers revolves around the fact that somewhat different patterns of deficit—the patterns mentioned above—will characterize the disorder at different ages. The examiner will therefore need to emphasize different tests, as a function of the age of the child being tested. Furthermore, although we would contend that most disabled readers presently pass through both phases, increased understanding of the disorder may make it possible to avoid many of the problems encountered in the later phase. For instance, failure to acquire certain reading strategies because of impoverished experience with reading might be remedied by teaching those strategies directly. We would also contend that disabled readers always pass through the earlier phase before entering the later phase; that is, one will not encounter older disabled readers with comprehension problems who never experienced decoding problems as beginning readers.

Test Materials Used With Disabled Readers

Our research involves elementary-age reading-disabled children, from first through sixth grades, whom we compare with normal readers of the same chronological age. All of the children are within the average range of intelligence or above, and any IQ differences between the groups are controlled in the statistical analyses. We give all of the children the same series of approximately eight or nine tests, two of which are standard psychometric tests, and the rest of which are measures we have developed ourselves, based on tasks used in information-processing research. The two psychometric tests are the reading comprehension subtest of a standardized reading test, such as the Nelson-Denny Reading Test or the Stanford Diagnostic Reading Test, and the Cattell Culture Fair Intelligence Test, a nonverbal test of intelligence. Both of these are group-administered measures.

The other tests are also group-administered, paper-and-pencil tasks. However, these experimental tasks tap specific areas of cognitive functioning thought to be relevant to reading disability. We have hypothesized that some of the cognitive functions tapped by these tasks will be deficient in disabled readers, whereas others will be intact. Except for one task, which was designed specifically to measure word decoding, the experimental measures require no reading, and very little writing. All instructions and test items are read aloud, and children give their responses by circling one of a group of multiple choices. None of the experimental tasks takes longer than 30 minutes to administer; several take as little as 10 to 15 minutes.

Over time, the composition of the set of experimental tasks has changed somewhat, as we have continued to refine certain tasks that appear to be particularly good at distinguishing disabled from normal readers, and as we have dropped other, less useful tasks. The tasks we are currently using tap the following areas; word decoding ability, ability to use context to determine the meanings of unfamiliar words, perceptual speed, phonemic and syllabic awareness, use of a speech-based code in short-term memory, and general language comprehension. We have selected one of these tasks, the one that measures phonemic and syllabic awareness, to explain in detail, as an example of a test that would be useful in cognitive assessment with disabled readers, particularly younger disabled readers. The test is very similar, but not identical, to a number of tasks that have been used in research with disabled readers (e.g., Mann & Liberman, 1982).

The Test of Syllable and Phoneme Counting consists of two parts (see Table 1). In the first part, children listen to a series of 15 words

Table 1

The Test of Syllable and Phoneme Counting

I.   Examiner says the following words aloud, and the children must circle the correct number of syllables that each word contains. The correct answer is given in parentheses next to each word.

Example words: but (1); butter (2); butterfly (3)

1. popsicle (3)   9. unexpectedly (5)

2. boat (1)   10. television (4)

3. motorcycle (4)   11. superintendent (5)

4. rattlesnake (3)   12. judge (1)

5. electricity (5)   13. green (1)

6. wagon (2)   14. waited (2)

7. babysitter (4)   15. spaghetti (3)

8. open (2)

II.   Here the children must tell the number of sounds, rather than the number of syllables, that each word contains. The examiner should tell children that some of the words will not be real words.

Example words: in (2); shin (3); spin (4)

1. fit (3)   9. grape (4)

2. smash (4)   10. dodge (3)

3. am (2)   11. band (4)

4. clump (5)   12. strap (5)

5. show (2)   13. tinch (4)

6. tree (3)   14. ome (2)

7. thrift (5)   15. plegs (5)

8. say (2)

spoken by the examiner. The task is to tell how many syllables are in each word. The number of syllables ranges from one (e.g., "boat") to five (e.g., "electricity"). The children indicate their responses by circling the correct number—1, 2, 3, 4, or 5—on an answer sheet. Only these numbers, and not the words read by the examiner, appear on the answer sheet.

The second part of the test is analogous to the first, except that here the children have to tell how many sounds (i.e., phonemes) there are in a series of words spoken by the examiner. All of the 15 words in the second portion of the test are one-syllable words. The number of sounds in each word ranges from two (e.g., "say") to five (e.g., "strap"). Again, children indicate their responses by circling a number on a page.

Several important points should be noted regarding the test. First, the two parts of the test appear to measure similar types of knowledge, but the syllabic awareness task is generally much easier for children than is the phonemic awareness task. Second, before each section, several examples are done with the children to ensure that they comprehend the nature of the task. It is vital for the examiner to be certain that the children have inferred the nature of the task from the examples, or the test will not be valid. Third, the number of sounds in a word is not necessarily synonymous with the number of letters in a word. For example, the word "show" has four letters, but only two sounds, those represented by the letters "sh" and "ow." The items for the second portion of the test were selected with this fact in mind, in order to avoid the possibility that children who could spell words might merely respond correctly by counting letters. For the same reason, several nonsense words were included as items at the end of the second part of the test. (Children are advised that some of the words will be nonsense words in the directions for this part of the test.)

Another type of task that has been used to measure phonemic or syllabic awareness is an elision task; the child is asked to say "carpenter" without the "car" (i.e., "penter") or "sharp" without the /sh/ (i.e., "arp"). However, the elision task is difficult to adapt to group administration without requiring children to write words, which is not a feasible alternative for poor or beginning readers. The advantage of our test is that it measures phonemic and syllabic awareness in a very practical format: the test can be administered to groups, requires no reading or spelling, takes only about 15 minutes to give, and is simple to score.

Implications of the Research for Cognitive Assessment

This line of experimental work illustrates a synthesis of information-processing and psychometric approaches to assessment. Both types of measures are used; the nonverbal IQ measure and the reading comprehension measure, which are used in classifying children as disabled or normal readers, constitute the psychometric measures, whereas the experimental tasks are the information-processing measures. Further, results from the two types of measures are integrated. For instance, we use the experimental tasks to give us some insights about why children might be classified as disabled readers; that is, we try to make inferences about the processes involved in reading disability based on the experimental tasks. Finally, the need for both types of measures is recognized in the basic philosophy that underlies our experimental work. Psychometric tests are not only required for qualifying youngsters for special services, but they have a degree of standardization and a history of use greatly lacking in most current information-processing measures. On the other hand, as we noted earlier, information-processing tasks also have something to add to assessment. Next, we will consider in detail what is to be gained from the use of information-processing tasks in the assessment of disabled readers, first in terms of our specific example, the Test of Syllable and Phoneme Counting, and then in more general terms.

Because there is considerable evidence that phonemic and syllabic awareness tasks are predictive of first-grade reading level (e.g., Helfgott, 1976; Mann & Liberman, 1982), the Test of Syllable and Phoneme Counting could be a useful addition to a kindergarten screening program for reading disability. There is also some evidence that training on various kinds of phonemic awareness tasks improves reading skill (Litcher & Roberge, 1979; Treiman & Baron, 1980; Williams, 1980). Thus, children who performed poorly on the test might well benefit from some type of syllabic and phonemic awareness training, particularly if this training were well-integrated with a comprehensive beginning reading program. Some examples of appropriate training activities would include syllable and phoneme counting activities; rhyming, alliterative, and Pig Latin games; and tasks involving the deletion or addition of a sound, such as the elision task described earlier. Further suggestions can be found in Engelmann (1969) and in Liberman and Shankweiler (1978).

Information-processing tasks also have something to add to the assessment of disabled readers in a more general sense. Currently, reading disability is generally defined in an exclusionary way, by establishing a discrepancy between overall intellectual ability and reading ability, in the absence of other handicapping conditions—hearing impairment, visual impairment, emotional disturbance, etc.—that could account for the discrepancy (*Federal Register*, December 29, 1977). However, a processing measure (or a set of measures) that identified disabled readers could simplify and increase the accuracy of identification procedures without resorting to an exclusionary criterion.

Furthermore, increased understanding of the processing deficits involved in reading disability could greatly improve instruction. Information-processing tasks often have clearer implications for training than do psychometric tests, because the former are oriented towards measurement of processes, and they tend to sample very specific areas of learning.

Even if some processes were not amenable to training, an increased understanding of the disorder might still benefit instruction in other ways. For example, earlier we suggested that the higher-level reading problems of older disabled readers are attributable not to a dysfunction in higher-level planning processes, but to other factors, such as lack of experience with reading or with certain academic demands. Disabled readers, for instance, may fail to induce certain study strategies because they do not have the kinds of experiences with text through which normal readers seem to induce and practice strategies. If this explanation is correct, then teaching those strategies directly would be helpful to disabled readers, not because they need training of higher-level planning processes (this kind of training has met with only limited success, anyway), but because their disabilities deprived them of the normal classroom opportunities to learn study strategies.

In addition, as we indicated at the beginning of the article, there is little emphasis on labeling youngsters according to the currently-used system of diagnostic categories (i.e., learning disabled, emotionally disturbed, mentally retarded, etc.) in the information-processing approach, thus avoiding some of the negative effects of labeling, such as lowered expectations. The use of psychometric tests to label youngsters according to these diagnostic categories is not an inevitable feature of the psychometric approach; rather, it is a function of how the approach has been used over many years. Nevertheless, because of this history of use, professionals, and even laypeople, tend to think in terms of these labels when they use psychometric tests. The information-processing approach, on the other hand, is not associated with this "excess baggage."

Finally, the kinds of group-administered, paper-and-pencil measures that we utilize are relatively simple to administer, score, and interpret, so that a wide range of service providers could employ them.

A Cautionary Note

There are potential difficulties with information-processing measures that should be noted by anyone interested in this type of assessment. First, the lack of standardization in these tests necessitates caution in their interpretation, especially when the same test is being used with children of various age levels. Poor performance on the test in a younger child may not indicate a processing deficit, but rather may mean that the test is simply too difficult for any youngster of that age.

Second, it is imperative that the tests be shown to relate to academic performance, as have the kinds of measures we have used as examples here, or they will not be providing information that is educationally relevant. Even when there is a relationship, service providers need to keep in mind that the relationship may not be causal in nature, and thus, training may not be warranted.

Third, even when training is warranted, it must be kept in mind that processes cannot be trained in isolation. Process training must be carefully integrated with more conventional academic instruction, and with training of other types of processes, such as higher-level planning processes.

Fourth, the fact that many different kinds of professionals can use cognitive assessment creates a need for caution in the administration and interpretation of the tests. There is always the danger that different professionals may give or interpret the same test differently, leading to confusion and misunderstanding.

Fifth, the tests are as unfamiliar to parents as they are to many professionals; thus, professionals not only must exercise care in using the tests, but they also must be able to interpret them clearly to parents.

Sixth, although the tests that we have used as examples here are short and practical, a battery of information-processing tasks that addressed a broad range of areas of cognitive functioning would be very time-consuming. Professionals would do best to use standard psychometric tests to assess broad areas of functioning, and limit their use of information-processing tasks to those specific areas that warrant more detailed assessment.

CONCLUSIONS

In this paper, we have described an approach to cognitive assessment with disabled readers that involves a synthesis of the traditional psychometric and the more recent information-processing approaches to assessment. In our approach, psychometric tests that are commonly used with the reading disabled, such as IQ and standardized reading tests, are supplemented by tasks adapted from information-processing research. As an example of one task, we described the Test of Syllable and Phoneme Counting. We concluded with a set of six cautionary guidelines for professionals who are interested in using information-processing measures in assessment.

Although this article focused upon one particular population, the reading disabled, the approach described here can be generalized to many different types of youngsters, including the mentally retarded and the gifted (Sternberg, in press; Sternberg & Spear, in press). With these other populations, the specific information-processing tasks that would be most useful might well differ from those suggested here, but the general principles of the approach would remain the same. In particular, examiners will need to keep in mind the strengths and weaknesses of information-processing measures, whatever child they test. Many of the weaknesses of these measures—lack of test standardization, lack of familiarity to parents and many professionals, and so forth—are tied to their newness, and may be remedied with the passage of time. The strengths of information-processing measures are connected largely to the fact that they are process-oriented. A more profound understanding of processes, with clearer implications for education, and less emphasis on an outmoded system of diagnostic classification, are some important elements that information-processing tasks can add to assessment.

REFERENCES

Crowder, R.G. (1982). *The psychology of reading*. New York: Oxford University Press.

Engelmann, S. (1969). *Preventing failure in the primary grades*. Chicago: Science Research Associates.

Federal Register (December 29, 1977). Procedures for evaluating specific learning disabilities. Washington, D.C.: Department of Health, Education, and Welfare.

Goffman, E. (1963). *Stigma: Notes on the management of spoiled identity*. Englewood Cliffs, N.J.: Prentice-Hall.

Helfgott, J. (1976). Phonemic segmentation and blending skills of kindergarten children: Implications for beginning reading acquisition. *Contemporary Educational Psychology, 1*, 157–169.

Ingalls, R.P. (1978). *Mental retardation: The changing outlook*. New York: Wiley and Sons.

Liberman, I.Y., & Shankweiler, D. (1978). Speech, the alphabet, and teaching to read. In L. Resnick & P. Weaver (Eds.), *Theory and practice of early reading*. New York: Wiley.

Litcher, J.H., & Roberge, L.P. (1979). First-grade intervention for reading achievement of high-risk children. *Bulletin of the Orton Society, 29*, 238–244.

MacMillan, D.L., Jones, R.L., & Aloia, G.F. (1974). The mentally retarded label: A theoretical analysis and review of research. *American Journal of Mental Deficiency, 79*, 241–261.

Mann, V.A., & Liberman, I.Y. (1982). *Phonological awareness and verbal short-term memory: Can they presage early reading problems?* Haskins Laboratories: Status Report on Speech Research SR-70.

Spear, L.C., & Sternberg, R.J. (in press). An information-processing framework for understanding reading disability. In S.J. Ceci (Ed.), *Handbook of cognitive, social, and neuropsychological aspects of learning disabilities* (Volume 2). Hillsdale, N.J.: Erlbaum.

Sternberg, R.J. (1977). *Intelligence, information processing, and analogical reasoning: The componential analysis of human abilities*. Hillsdale, N.J.: Erlbaum.

Sternberg, R.J. (in press). A unified theory of intellectual exceptionality. In J.G. Borkowski & J. Day (Eds.), *Cognition and intelligence in special children: Comparative approaches to retardation, learning disabilities, and giftedness*. Norwood, N.J.: Ablex.

Sternberg, R.J., & Spear, L.C. A triarchic theory of mental retardation. In N. Ellis & N. Bray (Eds.), *International Review of Research in Mental Retardation* (Volume 13). New York: Academic Press.

Treiman, R., & Baron, J. (1980). Segmental analysis ability: Development and relation to reading ability. In T. Waller & G. MacKinnon (Eds.), *Reading research: Advances in theory and practice, volume 2*. New York: Academic Press.

Williams, J.P. (1980). Teaching decoding with an emphasis on phoneme analysis and phoneme blending. *Journal of Educational Psychology, 72*, 1–15.

Learning Potential Assessment

Reuven Feuerstein
Yaacov Rand
Hadassah WIZO Canada Research Institute
Bar Ilan University

Mogens Jensen
Hadassah WIZO Canada Research Institute
Yale University

Shlomo Kaniel
David Tzuriel
Hadassah WIZO Canada Research Institute
Bar Ilan University

Nili Ben Shachar
Yael Mintzker
Hadassah WIZO Canada Research Institute

ABSTRACT. This article describes the foundations and uses of learning potential assessment, a dynamic method of determining the student's capacity for cognitive modifiability. The method, which forms the basis for the Learning Potential Assessment Device (LPAD), can assist in identifying low functioning students whose capacity for greater achievement typically goes undetected with traditional measures. Case studies of the use of the LPAD are presented.

This paper presents a dynamic approach to the assessment of cognitive modifiability in both individual and group settings and examines the philosophical and operational implications of this type of assessment approach.

The authors wish to acknowledge the important contribution made by Mr. Eitan Vig, the graphic artist at the Institute, in designing the LPAD materials. In addition, the authors acknowledge the vital support of the Hadassah WIZO Organization of Canada and its officers and the current President, Mrs. Cecily Peters.

Requests for reprints should be sent to Mogens Jensen, Department of Psychology, Yale University, Box 11A Yale Station, New Haven, CT 06520.

THE ASSUMPTION OF STATIC SYSTEMS:
SCHOOL AND CHILD

In order to meet present operating procedures school systems utilize tests and other measurement devices to generate information for classifying students, selecting students for participation in classes with limited enrollment, and measuring outcomes. The traditional use of tests and measurements is often guided by the basic assumptions that the school represents a static system embodying both status and goals, and that the successful student is the student whose functioning matches the requirements of the system. The degree of fit with the school system emerges as a central criterion for the assessment of the adequacy of the child's functioning. The emphasis is not on the identification of changes which the individual has—and eventually may be able—to undergo, but on the mere registration of the existent IQ, the existent repertoire of behaviors and motivation, and current knowledge of school skills.

This conception of the school as a static system is parallelled by the conception of the individual as a static system which cannot be modified. Consequently, assessment aims at the discovery of compatibilities and incompatibilities between two systems each of which essentially is perceived as immutable. Services rendered on the basis of such a conception of static systems will lead to very little other than a system of categorization of school vs. child and will not foster attempts either to create new systems in the school or new capacities in children. This system of categorization, in turn, refers children to particular schools or classes in order to increase as much as possible the "fit" between system and pupil.

THE ASSUMPTION OF OPEN SYSTEMS:
CHILD AND SCHOOL

In contradistinction to systems conceptualized as static, we would like to propose an alternative view characterized by a dynamic approach which considers both school system and child as highly modifiable through the double effects of life conditions and intervention. Within this orientation, support systems and services offered to the school employ dynamic approaches in all spheres of activity. In this approach, both goal setting and means of achieving goals are based on the perception of the individual as a modifiable, open system able to benefit from the school.

The belief that individuals are open and accessible to cognitive change is expressed in the theory of structural cognitive modifiability and the mediated learning experience, and in the three applied systems derived from it: the Learning Potential Assessment Device (a diagnostic-assessment system of cognitive modifiability), Instrumental Enrichment (a remediation program designed to bring about the realization of that potential for change), and, third, principles for establishing a "modifying" environment for the child in need (Feuerstein, 1979, 1980). From our point of view there is also reason to consider school systems as open and modifiable provided that the necessary conditions and prerequisites for change exist and are permitted to bear upon the school. Such prerequisites have to be established within the intrinsic need system governing the operation of school systems, and this need system must in turn reflect the need systems represented by child and family as well as those of the broader social, cultural, and economic context. In this vein, the services offered to school systems should function as agents for transmitting and responding to the need systems existing in the culture within which the school operates and to which the school has to adapt and cater.

The Significance of the Development of the Capacity to Change

An analysis of modern technological culture indicates that one of the most important conditions schools have to respond to is the need to develop the capacity of individuals to change. More specifically, we believe that no educational goal is more important than increasing the individual's capacity to modify his/her modalities of communication, body of knowledge, linguistic repertoire, skills repertoire and mores as a way of responding to the discontinuous, disruptive changes which characterize life today. Modifiability, or increases in the capacity to be modified, emerges in its own right as a major goal for educational systems. Much less important today is the inculcation of knowledge and knowledge about how knowledge is gathered. Both the actual information gathered and the way it is gathered may soon become obsolete. Investments in the sheer gathering, storing and retrieval of data may be meaningless considering the fact that the learner eventually will have to forget what has been learned and the way it was absorbed in favor of new content and innovative ways of communicating it.

Overall, it is the capacity to adapt to change, the capacity to acquire new modalities—rather than solely becoming automatized, crystallized and skillful in one particular modality—which must constitute the major, albeit not the sole, goal of education. Modifiability and its increase must be considered a major goal of school systems in order that they may adequately prepare students for the changing technological, economical, social and moral conditions with which they will be increasingly confronted.

From this point of view the dynamic assessment can play a very important role, both by providing data on the nature and extent of an individual's modifiability, and by defining the preferential ways and costs associated with its development. The dynamic, as contrasted with the static, approach to assessment postulates human modifiability as one of the most pervasive—and probably also most unique—characteristics of the human being. Specifically, human modifiability is considered possible irrespective of three conditions often considered as barriers to change: etiology, age, and severity of condition.

Etiology

Ensuring educational rights to all individuals regardless of etiological condition represents a very important achievement of the last decade. However, a general disbelief in the modifiability of individuals with certain endogenous conditions has frequently limited efforts to enhance their ability to adapt to changing conditions. The theory of structural cognitive modifiability postulates that endogenously determined conditions do not necessarily constitute immutable barriers. Indeed, our work shows that many individuals whose functioning is related to endogenous conditions are modifiable in many dimensions of their life (mental, emotional, and social) provided they receive the type of intervention which is required by their condition.

Age

Age has often been considered a barrier for modifiability in that critical periods have been postulated after which no further change of a structural nature can occur. It is a basic postulate of the theory of structural cognitive modifiability that *optimal* rather than *critical* periods should be considered to affect the development of individuals and that such optimal periods—given the possibility to vary the nature, extent, intensity and type of intervention—exist above and beyond biologically-determined periods of growth and development.

Severity of condition

Like etiology and age, severity of condition is invoked as a reason to consider an individual beyond reach as far as modifiability is concerned. Severity of condition certainly requires consideration of the nature and the amount of investment required, as well as the span of change which can be hoped for under specified conditions. However, severity of condition should not automatically be perceived as an immutable barrier which will *necessarily* prevent the attainment of higher levels of modifiability.

If this set of postulates is accepted, then the major goal of the assessment of individuals becomes the assessment of their modifiability rather than their present status. Modifiability, rather than present status, becomes the basis for predicting development, the basis for the setting of goals, and for identifying and providing the interventions upon which their realization may depend.

The shift from a static to a dynamic approach represents a shift from the concept of fixity and immutability of both intelligence and other characteristic traits of the individual to a view of the human being as a plastic, flexible and open system. The shift as one can see, is a function of philosophy and belief system, as well as a function of an awareness of needs and goals. Along with the postulates of the model, the theory, methodology, techniques and instruments of the Learning Potential Assessment Device (LPAD) have all been developed and empirically researched within such a framework of philosophy and awareness of need. Utilized during the last thirty years in Israel, the LPAD has been extremely helpful in modifying not only children's destinies but also educational systems.

DYNAMIC ASSESSMENT AND YOUTH ALIYA— PRELIMINARY COMMENTS

One of the educational systems which has been deeply affected by the LPAD and its underlying philosophy is Youth Aliya, an Israeli non-governmental agency, which has been faced with the absorption, placement and education of tens of thousands of children coming from large and deeply traumatized, high-risk populations of different cultural backgrounds, languages, cognitive styles, modalities of interaction with the environment, and modalities of schooling. Youth Aliya faced the need to ensure the adaptation of these children to the occidental, technological society prevailing in Israel. Many of these children, at age 14-15, functioned academically at a pre-operational level on Piagetian perceptual-motor tasks. On the basis of their performance on traditional static measures such as the Bender-Gestalt, the Binet-Simon, Wechsler-Bellevue, or Piaget-based tasks, the children could be considered to be organically disturbed, mentally retarded, or to function at irreversibly-low cognitive levels.

The use of the dynamic approach and the LPAD, details of which will be presented below, permitted educational policy-makers to reconsider the prevailing approaches to teaching these children. After the children's functioning was found to be highly modifiable, educational, social, and civil goals were set. These goals were very different from those suggested by their manifest low level of functioning and their declared IQ. Similarly, the LPAD identified the interventions necessary to achieve these goals in the varying conditions and contexts of these children's level of functioning. For many of those who came to Israel during the fifty years since the inception of Youth Aliah—among them survivors of the Holocaust and most recently children from Ethiopia—the dynamic approach represented a highly relevant paradigm. If assessed by static measures, these children would often be considered retarded with very little hope for a meaningfully modified level of functioning. The dynamic approach offers a very different conception—and hope—for them.

Changes in the Psychometric Approach Required by the Shift from Static to Dynamic Assessment

The shift from a static to a dynamic approach requires a number of basic changes in the psychometric approach. Contrary to some of those who became disenchanted with psychometric models in general and the static approach in particular, we consider the psychometric paradigm—with the necessary changes to render it dynamic—very important to retain. The psychometric paradigm uses a structured test situation for purposes of examining a sample of functions which will reflect a broader universe of functions. We consider this approach necessary, not just to provide an economic assessment of individuals, but also to set more remote educational goals and to prescribe and foster the particular conditions to attain them. Such alternative approaches as diagnostic teaching or naturalistic observation cannot be considered adequate to develop the information necessary to stipulate goals and conditions different from those based upon the individual's manifest level of functioning. We propose to keep the psychometric method but to render it dynamic through a number of basic changes in (1) instruments, (2) the nature of the test situation, (3) the goal of the assessment, and (4) the interpretation of results. The four changes required to produce a shift from static to dynamic assessment are briefly described below.

Instruments

The dynamic approach to assessment is a test-teach-test or, more accurately, test-mediate-test approach which attempts to produce structural change in the individual's registered level of functioning. The dynamic approach, in other words, does not merely seek to modify the amount and nature of information available to the individual, or the amount and nature of skills in the repertoire. Rather it first seeks to affect the individual's capacity to learn and to respond adequately to new situations and then to assess the extent of this change. This test-mediate-test method is very different from the test-coach-test approach which mainly is oriented towards producing certain units of information and then determining the extent to which these units are retained or have affected other units of information.

Opportunity for learning. A good test for the assessment of the modifiability of the individual will have different characteristics than those usually required for a good psychometric test instrument. Tests constructed for dynamic assessment must permit the examiner to assess modifiability and, on this basis, both predict future changes in the capacity to learn and determine the best conditions for developing this capacity. In order to accomplish this, the dynamic test instrument will be structured to offer opportunities for learning. The test will not merely constitute an opportunity for the examiner to register the examinee's responses but will also offer the examinee opportunitites to be taught and modified by this teaching.

Tasks and questions used in static tests for the most part do not lend themselves to the necessary types of mediational and teaching interaction required by dynamic assessment. One cannot really modify the individual by giving him or her the answer to the question: "Who is the President of the United States?" One can tell the answer to the examinee, it may or may not be retained, but even if retained this will not meaningfully affect those areas which constitute the criteria for an assessment of the examinee's modifiability. The same is true of certain types of non-verbal tasks. Simply offering the examinee the answer will affect meaningfully neither the examinee's capacity to succeed better on the next task nor the examiner's knowledge of what the modifiability of the child may be. For dynamic assessment, tests will have to be constructed which permit the examinee to learn something which will *affect learning capacity* and thus efficiency in handling new tasks.

Sensitivity to change. A second condition which a test in a dynamic assessment must fulfill is sensitivity to change. In an assessment of modifiability the test instruments must function as detectors of newly-acquired functions, concepts, principles, vocabulary, attitudes and motivation. Very sensitive instruments are needed because the changes produced in the individual often will not reach a magnitude where they are immediately obvious. The types of tasks usually employed in psychometric tests are not sufficiently sensitive to permit the examiner to detect, interpret and ascribe a predictive value to each minimal change produced within the short period of the dynamic assessment. In contrast, the LPAD tasks are structured and organized to act as detectors of modifiability.

Successful interaction. Another important characteristic of dynamic tests is the opportunity they must provide for the examinee to interact successfully with tasks and experience the feeling of growing competence. Tasks should be neither too simple nor too familiar. Too much familiarity prevents a feeling of challenge and of competency. The level of complexity should create a challenge, a feeling of competency following successful mastery, and be such that it creates within the individual enough affinity with other tasks to make transfer possible.

The three characteristics of opportunity for learning, sensitivity to change, and successful interaction for the development of competence have been conceptualized in the model presented in Figure 1. The center represents a task which has been determined to

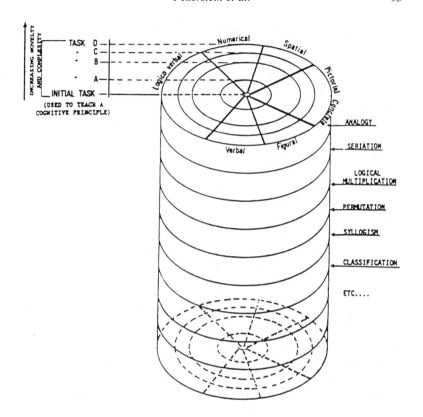

Figure 1. The LPAD model for construction of dynamic tests

be inaccessible to the examinee and hence to require special intervention. This intervention is given in the form of a mediational interaction. This interaction entails, as a result of the examiner's intentionality, the awareness on the part of the individual that he or she is taught not just this particular task but a transcending principle which reaches out to equip the examinee with the prerequisite which will enable him or her to learn similar and progressively more difficult tasks. The mediational interaction entails the attribution of a meaning to this particular task in order to enhance the motivation of the individual and his or her readiness to become involved with it. It entails the use of cognitive modalities for regulating behavior, i.e., inhibition and control of impulsivity and acceleration of responses. The examiner teaches the individual how to consider the interaction with the task as a function of present competency and degree of task difficulty, thus permitting the regulation of investments in the perceptual process and the elaboration of the collected information. This entails developing and mediating a feeling of competence by interpreting the performance to the child, limiting the import of failure, and enabling the child to succeed. The mediational interaction involves a need to share and to communicate findings as well as the correction of deficient functions on the output level. In these and other ways the examiner will attempt to modify the individual's functioning structurally.

Following the mediational interaction, tasks are offered to the individual to detect and show the examinee the kinds of changes which have occurred in the course of the mediational interaction. Based on progressively more remote and unfamiliar variations of the task used for the mediational interaction, these tasks are used to collect evidence of the individual's modifiability, that is, the capacity to use experience in order to adapt to progressively new situations.

As Figure 1 shows, the assessment, following the mediational interaction, can progress out from the center, assessing changes in the same type of task across languages of presentation (e.g., figural or numerical). Alternatively, it can move down the axis so that the effects of mediation on the individual's mastery of tasks taken from different kinds of mental operations (e.g., analogical reasoning, syllogistic reasoning, inferential thinking, inductive or deductive reasoning) are assessed. Figure 2 shows examples of tasks from the LPAD which can be utilized to provide mediation and subsequently assess modifiability.

The dynamic use of tests of this kind has results very different from those obtained with tests structured according to the conventional psychometric model. Through the LPAD, we seek to determine: (1) to what extent an individual who may have manifested great difficulties in certain types of tasks will be able to master them; (2) how much investment is necessary to produce such mastery; (3) what the meaning of this acquisition is in terms of the child's capacity to master tasks similar to the one mastered with the help of the mediator; (4) what types of investments will be necessary to produce transfer of otherwise known relationships, and their application in new and progressively more unfamiliar situations; and (5) what the most effective ways to produce the desired changes are with reference to each individual's condition, experience, and

L.P.A.D Set-Variations

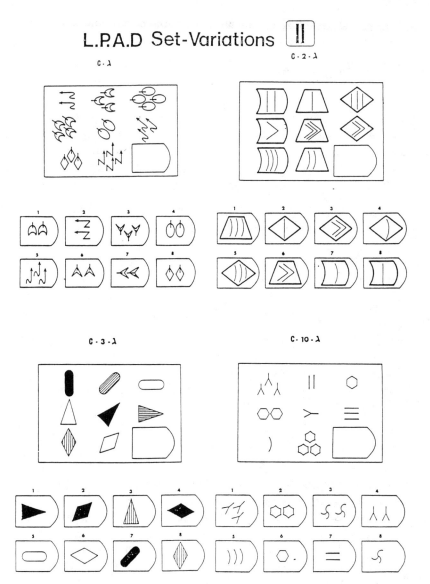

Figure 2. Examples of tasks from the LPAD which can be utilized to provide mediation and subsequently assess modifiability.

educational-cognitive equipment. Prescriptive teaching is a direct outcome of such an approach.

Test Situation (Examiner-Examinee Relationship)

A second and radical change required to produce the shift from a static to a dynamic psychometric approach is a change in the test situation. The conventional psychometric approach standardizes the test situation. Uniformity of test presentation for all children is deemed necessary to ensure that results will reflect capacity rather than contingencies of task presentation and to ensure comparability across individual respondents. This emphasis upon comparability as a sine qua non condition for predictability runs parallel to the view of the school as a static, fixed and immutable system unable to adapt to the individual.

In the conventional psychometric approach, accordingly, the examiner is not supposed to offer feedback to the examinee about the amount and nature of experienced success, reveal any element of functioning necessary for successful mastery at follow-up, or even permit the child to become more acquainted or familiar with the tasks. The whole test situation is strongly shaped and confined to prescribed interaction which cannot possibly respond to the needs of the child, especially the one with learning difficulties. Indeed, the lack of feedback, the lack of meaningful encouragement, the inability of the examiner to provide help when needed may cause the child to cease responding so that existing capacities, skills and informational repertoires are not revealed.

The shift to a dynamic approach totally changes the examiner-examinee relationship. The LPAD requires that the examiner function as a teacher-mediator: The examiner does not wait for the child to fail but performs the utmost to prevent failure. From cues provided by the child, the examiner anticipates results and intervenes to prevent failure by changing inappropriate behaviors. The exmainer can make the child attend better, and offer opportunity to sharpen perception and gather data in ways appropriate for their elaboration.

In this type of interaction the examiner's role (often stressed with statements such as "I will help you") is that of a participant who does indeed provide the child with help. By creating conditions for focusing, for understanding the broader meaning of a task, and for successful interaction with it, the examiner creates a climate in which the child's capacity to approach new tasks is enhanced.

In sum, the goals of the LPAD test situation include: (1) the correction of deficient functions; (2) the regulation of behavior to inhibit passivity and enhance the child's capacity to initiate responses; (3) the creation of insight; (4) the formulation of principles, results, and methods which enable the child to approach tasks presented later on; (5) the production of a feeling of competence; and (6) the production of the feeling of being a generator rather than reproducer of information.

Assessment Goals: Process Orientation

In the LPAD, the interest of the examiner is mainly centered around the *process* responsible for the nature of the response produced by the child. The shift from a product to a process orientation is greatly facilitated by the analysis of the examinee's functioning using the list of deficient functions and the cognitive map. The cognitive map is a conceptual tool which enables the examiner to carry out a systematic assessment of the contribution of various task components to the errors and deficiencies shown by the examinee in interaction with the task. Using the cognitive map, the examiner searches for the locus of the child's failure and identifies the preferential ways to overcome the deficiencies shown. Failure may be due to the particular *content* presented to the child, which may be more or less familiar (familiarity being a function of the cultural context in which the child has been raised and the types of experience he or she has been exposed to), or due to the particular *language* in which it was presented. Alternatively, the child's capacity to function on a particular task may be related to characteristics of the task where too heavy a burden may be placed on *cognitive functions* involved in the collection of information (input, e.g., blurred and sweeping perception; unplanned, impulsive, and unsystematic explorative behavior; impaired spatial and temporal orientation), the mental transformation of information (elaboration, e.g., lack of spontaneous comparative behavior; narrowness of the psychological field; lack of orientation towards the need for logical evidence), or in the communication of the elaborated response (output, e.g., blocking; impaired verbal tools; deficiency of visual transport). There is also the possibility that the child's failure may be due to the unavailability of a required *operation* (e.g., analogical reasoning, syllogistic thinking) or the failure may be related to the *complexity* of the task, where the number of units of information to be handled simultaneously may exceed the child's current capacity. In addition, the *level of abstraction* may not be appropriate either because of developmental stage or the child's previous experience. Failure, finally, may be due to impaired or simply *underdeveloped efficiency* which can mask the child's ability to function at higher levels.

The cognitive map, with its seven parameters (content, language, phase of the mental act, operations, complexity, abstractness and efficiency), and the list of the deficient functions is of the greatest importance in the shift from product to process. The process, once understood, may enable us to interpret in a very different way the successes and failures of the individual. In addition it may equip us with indications about goals which can be set for the child if and when certain specified conditions of failure are corrected by proper intervention.

Interpretation of Results

Interpretation of results in the traditional psychometric mode is characterized by the need to create a global index of mental functioning. In doing so, very little attention is given to those isolated, outstanding types of answers which appear almost unpredictably and therefore cannot be considered typical of the examinee's functioning. Usually these outstanding answers, whether exceptionally brilliant or exceptionally dysfunctional, are ignored. Often considered a random aberration, the outstandingly good answer, in particular, is thought to be of little relevance for determining the way the individual functions. This is true. Such answers do not play an important role in the individual's present functioning where they may be episodic. However, the fact that they appear occasionally or even only once is to be interpreted as reflecting a capacity which is not more frequently manifested in the individual's behavior for a variety of possible reasons. In static psychometric testing outstandingly good answers are neither encouraged nor given opportunities to appear. In many cases the very fact that an individual has failed one or more times on a particular type of task may constitute the point of deciding not to offer more advanced questions or tasks.

In the LPAD the appearance of such peaks of functioning are encouraged, sought after, and taken as indicators of higher levels of functioning which, with proper intervention, may become more typical. This type of interpretation creates new working hypotheses. Rather than pointing out the individual's inadequacies, these working hypotheses ensure that the examiner's interaction with the examinee will be animated by the need to search for and foster the development of the capacities which are indicated by these peak responses.

YOUTH ALIYA—
HISTORICAL SOURCES OF EVIDENCE

As indicated earlier, Youth Aliya was faced with tens of thousands of low functioning children who came to Israel from various parts of the world. Static test instruments proved unable to distinguish between those children whose incapacity to respond to certain types of tasks was due to cultural difference and those whose incapacity was due to the phenomenon of cultural deprivation—a pervasive phenomenon among these children due to a wide variety of conditions which may contribute to the inadequate development of cognitive functioning.

The use of the LPAD became imperative because static measures not only did not distinguish between the etiological conditions of these children but, even more important, did not indicate what had to be done for those in need of special care. The use of the LPAD did not serve simply a selection function, but was used rather to determine *what kind of help* each child needed to receive. To do so it was of the greatest importance *not* to use the manifest level of functioning considering that it tells very little about what the individual will be able to do if and when the necessary adaptation tools are offered. We argued with educators and policy makers responsible for the program that any child, irrespective of what made him or her function so low, should be given the opportunity to be assessed with a dynamic approach. Decisions about placement, moreover, should be made on the basis of the child's modifiability rather than on the basis of etiology or the child's present level of functioning.

The possibility of showing that what was currently inaccessible to the child can be made accessible with fairly brief (5 to 10 hours) intervention enabled educators to set very different goals for these children. Our ability to point to achievements in the test situation and show change produced through mediational intervention, gave credibility to our declarations about these children despite the fact that our statements were at variance with their manifest levels of functioning.

This credibility literally enabled us to change the course of life for many thousands of children. More important, it also brought about a total change in the attitude of policy makers within the Youth Aliya organization. This attitudinal change opened the gates of mainstreamed education to tens of thousands of youngsters previously considered in need of special education. Indeed, the impact on teachers and educational systems in absorption centers, youth villages, kibbutzim, and urban residential centers affiliated with Youth Aliya permitted these children to avoid being placed, treated and educated on the basis of their manifest levels of functioning.

The Preparatory Classes Study

In 1958 we were asked to contribute to the establishment of an absorption center for totally or functionally illiterate children with IQ's in the 50-75 range. Candidates for the program were assessed with the LPAD and the program itself largely reflected the findings on these children. A large variety of levels of functioning were observed with great variations in the capacity to attain certain types of cognitive functioning (e.g., analogical reasoning, simple math), attention span, socialization and emotional responsiveness.

The goal of the program was to secure the integration of the students, after proper investments, into the normal Youth Aliya population in the kibbutzim, youth villages and other schools (high schools, vocational and academic schools). The program was structured as a period of intensive preparation which took into account the types of schools awaiting referral, the kinds of children with whom they would become associated, and the diversity of need systems to which they would be exposed. The preparation for such an integrational goal had to take into account many dimensions of cognitive functioning and socialization.

Since 1958, more than 15,000 children have been accepted into these preparatory programs with subsequent successful integration into regular educational and vocational programs as well as into the Israeli army. Figure 3 presents results obtained by the Israeli army at induction for youngsters who benefited from the preparatory program (including Instrumental Enrichment—a planned curricu-

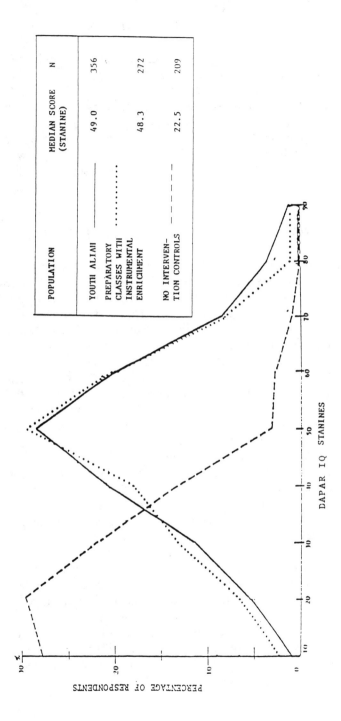

Figure 3. Results obtained on the DAPAR IQ test for students participating in Instrumental Enrichment two comparison groups.

lum designed to target deficient cognitive functions and need systems through the provision of mediating learning experiences in the classroom). For purposes of comparison, Figure 3 also presents data for a random sample of normal functioning Youth Aliya graduates and for a group of untreated youngsters similar in demographic and background data to those in the preparatory classes. The data suggest that this group of youngsters was meaningfully affected by the investments indicated necessary by the LPAD.

GROUP TESTING WITH THE LPAD

The major application of the Learning Potential Assessment Device is in the assessment of modifiability in the individual case. There the assessment of modifiability is carried out in a very thorough, systematic, and complete way. However, this particular application of the LPAD has two disadvantages. The first is that it requires a large investment of time. Secondly, the provision of maximal rather than optimal conditions produces evidence of modifiability which does not always reflect the conditions in which individuals will find themselves in extracurricular situations, in the classroom, or even in their interactions with a tutor. Furthermore, the individually applied LPAD may pose logistical and methodological difficulties for certain research purposes.

Although less clinically systematic—and offering much less information—group testing with the LPAD may for these reasons have some important advantages especially when systems have to assess a large number of individuals. Under these conditions group testing may not only be legitimate, but may hold some advantages over individualized assessment as it more closely approximates the types of conditions learners experience in a classroom.

The individualized format of the LPAD can be limited to those children who prove unable to benefit from the more circumscribed mediational intervention offered in the context of group testing. Those who do benefit from the group testing must certainly be considered to have high modifiability under all, or nearly all, conditions. Those who have not been able to benefit from the group test situation are likely to need a different investment whose parameters must be carefully determined through individualized assessment.

Screening with the LPAD group-test allows the dynamic assessment process to be used. Among other important features, the process orientation is retained in the LPAD group test where one can learn which cognitive functions have been deficient and which are responsible for the errors observed. Changes produced by the mediational process in the individual's functioning are assessed by the test and this evidence of modifiability is then translated into a prescription designed to fit the needs of each particular child.

The entire approach is geared to identifying and setting goals for the individual's development which are different from those which would be set on the basis of conventional test results. Such an approach to the individual will, if adopted, of necessity change the school system. The individual will not be considered for acceptance or rejection at a particular school only on the basis of current performance. Instead, the different goals and avenues to achieve them arrived at through dynamic assessment will influence schools to embark upon intervention programs which previously were considered superfluous.

THE HODAYOT STUDY: HOMOGENEITY AND ABILITY GROUPING IN CLASSROOM FORMATION— QUESTIONING THE LEGITIMACY

This study illustrates the use of the LPAD as a group test and its value in creating more optimal conditions for the development of low functioning children. The study was commissioned by the educators of a vocational high school where two groups of children were placed. One group was comprised of normal functioning students who were expected to matriculate. The other group consisted of students who were offered a watered-down type of instructional program because of their allegedly low (borderline to EMR range) IQ—and their low level of scholastic achievement.

The educational staff was distressed by the unexpected observation that youngsters placed in the lower program were socially well-adapted and also showing adequate functioning in certain areas of vocational studies. This observation, in conjunction with the finding that these students showed little motivation for academic studies—and the fact that teachers soon stopped requiring any meaningful academic involvement from them—made the staff question the legitimacy and usefulness of the homogenous placement based on the "ability grouping". Expressing doubts about the extent to which the manifest level of functioning and the IQ reflected the true capacities of these students, the staff commissioned the dynamic assessment with the LPAD group test. The purpose of the assessment was to go beyond the manifest level of functioning and learn to what extent the benefits of the educational system could be enhanced for these children by placing them among their higher functioning peers under controlled conditions for instruction.

The results of the LPAD group test and follow-up evaluation (see Table 1) indicated not only that the merging of these students with their higher functioning peers was legitimate but also that great benefits were obtained for the low functioning population with very little if any risk for the higher functioning students. Follow-up data collected at the time students were drafted into the army indicated that the differences initially registered between the groups had almost totally disappeared. Moreover, a comparison between higher functioning children participating in the merger and similar youngsters not merged with low functioning peers revealed no differences between the groups. The higher functioning students, in other words, were not found to be disadvantaged by the merger. The results point to the usefulness of the LPAD for identifying the high degree of modifiability in students regardless of their low manifest level of functioning and for helping educators structure groups and programs to achieve outcomes reflecting the true capacities of these students.

In a current study, the LPAD group test is utilized to assist schools which hitherto have had little success in promoting students to higher levels of academic achievement. The project was initiated by the Israel Ministry of Education due to concern for certain schools showing very low numbers of students reaching matriculation. As is often the case, the tendency has been to explain this failure in terms of the nature of the population of students: its ethnic make-up, the environmental conditions, the parental values and levels of education.

In a pilot study which we carried out in targeted schools, children referred to special education were individually assessed with the LPAD. The results indicated that these children were able to learn at levels much higher than those to which they had been referred. Following the pilot study, the Ministry of Education asked us to use the LPAD in two schools to question conventional assumptions

Table 1

The Hodayot Study: The Effects of Mainstreaming Low-Functioning Students Based on Dynamic Assessment

	Grade 9							Grade 10						
	Students in Low Ability Group		Students in Regular Group		Test of Significance			Students in Low Ability Group		Students in Regular Group		Test of Significance		
Measure	Mean	S.D.	Mean	S.D.	t	df	p	Mean	S.D.	Mean	S.D.	t	df	p
Before regrouping														
PMA1	165.9	17.8	153.8	14.7	3.00	65	.01	170.3	14.9	154.3	22.6	3.22	57	.01
(n)	(32)		(35)					(36)		(23)				
One year after regrouping:														
PMA2	189.6	12.7	179.6	13.5	2.78	51	.01	190.5	11.2	183.3	20.3	1.55	46	NS
(n)	(28)		(27)					(32)		(16)				
At Army induction:														
DAPAR	57.3	10.7	52.4	10.3	1.64	53	NS	57.4	13.6	51.3	18.6	1.12	40	NS
KABA	46.4	8.2	44.8	8.2	0.75	53	NS	44.2	10.4	40.3	10.5	1.06	40	NS
Hebrew	7.8	0.9	7.4	1.0	1.58	53	NS	7.8	1.1	7.6	1.6	0.50	40	NS
(n)	(30)		(25)					(27)		(15)				

regarding low levels of functioning, focusing instead upon the school system, its expectations, curriculum, and enrichment programs. The results of LPAD group testing were presented to the principals, the educational staff, the children, and parents. Consultation, training in cognitive modifiability, in Instrumental Enrichment and in the use of mediated learning experiences became accepted and even desired by teachers.

This was followed by an intensive period of additional research and consultation which was oriented toward the goal of affecting the educational *systems* and not merely the low functioning, retarded students within them. These efforts have meaningfully affected the total school system previously plagued by a pessimistic view of the prospects for these children. The confrontation with the results obtained in the LPAD—a confrontation often produced through direct observations of LPAD sessions—changed dramatically the deeply ingrained doubts of educators offering them new ways of approaching the children in their care. Additional work with the parents has created an awareness of their role and their rights to require a more active approach in promoting the welfare of their children.

Another use of the LPAD is illustrated by a project, also commissioned by the Israel Ministry of Education, where the LPAD is used to detect gifted children among low functioning students. About 1300 children have been examined with the LPAD group test in this project. The children detected as gifted receive an intensive intervention program currently offered by Bar-Ilan University.

As suggested by these examples there is a great diversity of application for both the individual and the group LPAD and they all converge toward the attempt to modify both the child and the school system in order to promote higher levels of functioning.

REFERENCES

Feuerstein, R. (1979). *The dynamic assessment of retarded performers: The Learning Potential Assessment Device, theory, instruments, and techniques.* Baltimore: University Park Press.

Feuerstein, R. (1980). *Instrumental enrichment: An intervention program for cognitive modifiability.* Baltimore: University Park Press.

Neuropsychological Assessment

Lawrence C. Hartlage

Medical College of Georgia

ABSTRACT. Although it has been known for more than a hundred years that subtle damage to specific brain areas can result in reading, listening comprehension, and expressive speech problems, the topic of brain-behavior relationships has only recently become of interest to psychologists and others serving children with learning problems. Comprehensive batteries for neuropsychological assessment of children, such as the Reitan-Indiana and Luria-Nebraska Children's Batteries, have demonstrated diagnostic validity, with agreement between findings on the two Batteries in the range of 90%. For those wishing to assess some aspects of children's neuropsychological functioning without the use of a comprehensive battery, guidelines are proposed for the neuropsychological interpretation of assessment instruments commonly used by school psychologists and educational diagnosticians.

Many behaviors of interest to those who provide special services in school settings depend on neurological substrates. Learning, for example, whether it involves sensation, perception, or memory, is a neurological phenomenon, and selective disorders or impairments in learning have been shown to result from fairly circumscribed areas of neurological impairment.

For several reasons, many of which appear to reflect traditional content in the training of school psychologists and educational diagnosticians, the assessment of neurological function in school settings has been treated as extrinisic to school practice. Brain injury, for example, is commonly viewed as an end-point diagnosis, rather than as a working hypothesis in the evaluation of etiologic possibilities underlying learning or behavior problems. For children viewed in terms of a dichotomous brain-injured vs. normal continuum, those with suspected brain injury are typically referred for

---

Requests for reprints should be sent to: Lawrence C. Hartlage, Neuropsychology Division, Medical College of Georgia, Augusta, GA 30902.

external evaluation, either to a neurologist or to a psychologist specializing in neuropsychological assessment. The identification of such children as brain injured by school diagnostic personnel may be based on some pathognomonic sign, such as impaired performance on visual motor tests or Wechsler Scale asymmetry, and usually involves the perception of neurological impairment as a diagnostic conclusion rather than a piece in the tapestry of each individual's unique configuration of cognitive strengths and weaknesses.

An alternative approach, which in recent years has been gaining support, involves the use of common standardized psychological measures to develop working hypotheses concerning the relative functional efficiency of discrete cortical systems (e.g., Hartlage, 1975, 1979, 1984a). In this conceptual approach, data from common psychometric instruments, coupled with developmental history and behavioral data, and occasionally from measures involving sensory and motory functions, are synthesized into inferential statements concerning the possible neurological substrates of learning or adjustment problems. It is this combination of psychological assessment strategies which gave use to the term neuropsychology. A brief description of this discipline and its rationale and procedures may help put this approach in a more appropriate context.

A RATIONALE
FOR NEUROPSYCHOLOGICAL ASSESSMENT

For more than a hundred years it has been known that discrete higher mental functions such as verbal fluency or comprehension of spoken language depend on discrete areas of the cortex (e.g., Broca, 1863; Wernicke, 1874); before the beginning of the present century both English and German physicians had identified cortical areas apparently necessary for fluent reading. Unfortunately, early attempts to relate neurological phenomena to educational intervention were not successful (e.g., Delacato, 1959, 1963, 1966; Orton, 1928, 1937). One major limitation involved the fact that studies of disordered brain function depended on pathological (e.g., autopsy) confirmation, and so were not readily applicable to educational intervention. More recent research, augmented by developments in electrophysiology, neurodiagnostic imaging and other sophisticated neuropsychological procedures, has greatly alleviated the problem of studying functioning in vitro, to the point where modern neuropsychology has a number of implications for school settings. An illustrative example, involving the measurement of cerebral asymmetry, may help show how attention to the neurological substrates of learning may be of relevance to both diagnosis and intervention in the schools.

It is now well recognized that in human beings the cerebral hemispheres have differential facility for given mental processes, with the left (dominant) cerebral hemisphere commonly more efficient in verbal tasks and in processing information in logical, sequential, analytic ways. Conversely, the right (nondominant) hemisphere is generally more efficient on spatial tasks and for processing information in wholistic, intuitive, gestalt-like ways. It has been demonstrated that cerebral asymmetry is present in approximately 77% of human beings (Geschwind & Levitsky, 1968) and further shown that this asymmetry is present in the same percentage and extent well before birth (Chi, Dooling, & Gilles, 1977; Galaburda, LeMay, Kemper, & Geschwind, 1978). Thus cerebral asymmetry appears to represent a fairly constant condition not determined by environmental phenomena.

In light of the relative stability of cerebral asymmetry over the life span, the specialization of certain functions within the hemispheres, involving greater left hemispheric specialization for language and sequential processing and greater right hemispheric specialization for spatial and simultaneous information processing, has some fairly obvious implications for special educational diagnostic and intervention approaches. The implications evolve from the assumption that there is a relationship between anatomic and functional asymmetry: presumably a child with asymmetry favoring the left cerebral hemisphere would have better proficiencies with language-mediated tasks (e.g., possible higher verbal than performance IQ); would process information more efficiently if presented in a linguistic as opposed to a spatial mode; and could perform better using a sequential as opposed to simultaneous problem-solving strategy. There is fairly compelling evidence for this presumption from persons with extreme differences in hemispheric processing ability. The vast majority of children with autism, for example, present clear neuroradiologic evidence of inadequate development of the left hemisphere areas involved with language, and demonstrate inability to establish effective verbal communication (e.g., Kanner, 1943; Hauser, DeLon & Rosman, 1975), although some success has been demonstrated in teaching sign language to them

(Bonivillion, Nelson, & Ryne, 1981). Similarly, for many years children and adults with documented damage to certain right hemisphere areas have demonstrated clear deficits on tests of spatial functions and with aspects of simultaneous thinking (e.g., Semmes, 1968; Smith, 1966), although language and sequential thinking processes are intact (e.g., Warrington, James, & Kinsbourne, 1966). In less extreme cases, recent research has shown that instruction which focuses on the favored hemisphere, as assessed by physiological measures of asymmetry, is more effective than instruction focused on the nonfavored one (e.g., Hartlage, 1984c).

Thus a neuropsychological approach to assessment and intervention with special children differs from more traditional psychoeducational assessment in at least three important ways. First, it attempts to determine why a given child has learning difficulty. Second, it produces findings which are verifiable by independent external criteria, such as electrophysiologic or neuroradiologic procedures (e.g., specialized electroencephalogram, nuclear magnetic resonance, computerized axial tomography, positron emission tomography, or regional cerebral blood flow studies). Finally, it proposes intervention approaches based on verifiable biological constructs combined with hypothetical psychological constructs congruent with the biological ones, as opposed to only hypothesized psychological constructs.

PROCEDURES
FOR NEUROPSYCHOLOGICAL ASSESSMENT

Neuropsychological assessment to verify the existence of brain impairment is most likely to involve the use of a standardized battery, the most common and venerable of which are the Reitan-Indiana Neuropsychological Test Battery for children 5–8 years, and the Halstead-Reitan Neuropsychological Test Battery for children ages 9–14 years (Selz, 1981), or the Luria-Nebraska Neuropsychological Battery for children ages in the 8–12 year old range (Golden, 1981; Wilkening, 1981). The Reitan and Luria Children's Batteries are basically revisions or downward extensions of the adult batteries bearing the same names (Berg, Bolter, Ch'ien, Williams, Lancaster, & Cummings, 1983), which have been found to be equally valid for the identification of brain damage in adults (Golden, Kane, Sweet, Moses, Cardellino, Templeton, Vicente, & Graham, 1981; Moses &

Golden, 1979). A brief description of the background and characteristics of the Reitan and Luria Batteries may help identify their
diagnostic and interpretive implications for school setings.

The Reitan Battery is based on a revision of an original battery
developed by a psychologist, Ward Halstead, and contains a number
of independent measures of psychological functions, arranged into
tests with at least ordinal scaling characteristics. The approximately
two-dozen tests include fluid aspects of cognitive functions, with
fairly complex integration required on many of the measures. There
is a heavy emphasis on intellective functions, with approximately
80% of the items reflecting measures of abilities believed to be
primarily mediated by one or the other cerebral hemisphere, and
approximately 20% of the items reflecting abilities believed to
involve both cerebral hemispheres. The Battery does not lend itself
to partial or abbreviated use, because each test within the Battery is
considered to contribute information concerning brain-behavior
relationships in an interdependent way. As there are no norms for
easy interpretation of findings, the user must have considerable
sophistication in analyzing results based on thorough knowledge of
the functions measured by each scale. Time required for administration and scoring can involve up to eight hours.

The Luria Children's Battery is based on Luria's neurological
examination procedure, and consists of 149 items taken from the
269 item adult Battery. Each item is scored on an 0–2 scale, with the
higher score representing inability to perform the item. Items are
arranged into eleven major subscales. The items tend to emphasize
simple, crystallized abilities, with fairly discrete aspects of function
measured by most items. There is a special focus on language, with
the majority of items centered on some aspects of this function.
With respect to cortical areas, there is better coverage of functions
believed to be mediated by the left cerebral hemisphere, with less
emphasis directed to abilities believed to involve the right hemisphere, and much less emphasis on presumably bilateral hemispheric functioning. Some modification in standard administration
may be feasible. A decision-tree approach, whereby the most
complex tasks within content groupings are administered first, with
credit given to simpler items within the 48 cluster decision tree, has
been demonstrated to be valid for use with the full (adult) Battery
(Webster & Dostrou, 1982; Webster, Dostrou & Scott, 1983), and
presumably this approach may be adaptable to the children's
version. Scores for the major subscales are convertible to T-scores,

with a mean of 50 and standard deviation of 10. Time required for administration and scoring can involve approximately three hours. Research has shown 91% agreement between the two children's Batteries, suggesting that they may be grossly comparable in the differentiation of cerebral dysfunction (Berg, Bolter, Ch'ien, Williams, Lancaster, & Cummings, 1984). There are several differences between the batteries, however, which may commend one or the other as being especially relevant for use in given situations. The Luria Children's Battery has a clear advantage involving time required for administration, especially if a decision-tree approach is used. It is limited in detecting subtle changes in a child, as might be required in assessing treatment efficiency or a decline in functioning, since the 0–2 scoring range for each item makes it difficult to detect subtle differences. Further, there is occasionally heterogeneity of items within the subscale grouping, so that diagnostic conclusions based on profile configurations need to be interpreted with caution. The memory scale, for example, contains both verbal and nonverbal items and may fail to reveal nonverbal deficits in children with superior verbal memory skills. The Battery's thorough coverage of language makes it helpful for evaluating children with language-based learning disorders (e.g., Geary, Jennings, Schultz, & Alpes, 1984), although its tendency to measure fairly simple, crystallized aspects of functioning may present difficulties for predicting how a child processes more dynamic, complex information in an educational context. For the sophisticated clinician, findings can be enhanced by a qualitative interpretation of the results (e.g., Golden, 1981). For the diagnostician without formal training in brain-behavior relationships, the apparently straightforward T-score profile is appealing, but can result in both false positive and false negative errors if interpretation of a given child's performance is based solely on the profile.

The Children's versions of the Reitan Battery, with its fairly precise scoring system and considerable range of scores for most tests, lends itself to the detection of subtle changes such as might be induced by the initiation of drug therapy or by a slowly degenerative disease process. This sensitivity, however, is achieved at the cost of a fairly extensive time commitment by both the child and examiner. Because there is no specific test of discrete abilities, considerable inferential and diagnostic skill is required for valid conclusions to be reached about discrete abilities and their neuropsychological substrates. Further, the fairly complex nature of many of the tests requires considerable clinical skill in interpretation, because poor performance on a given item can involve more than one cortical area or functional system. The fairly balanced sampling of areas believed to be subserved by both hemispheres makes the Battery sufficiently comprehensive for assessing most types of cortical dysfunctions. The fluid and complex nature of abilities assessed with measures such as the Categories Test permits insights into the child's dynamic process of hypothesis generating and testing, but may be sensitive to such factors as depression, confusion, or sedation, and like most tests in the Battery, needs to be viewed in the context of the child's global performance on all measures. This battery, perhaps to an extent considerably greater than involved with the Children's Luria, requires considerable sophistication in both administration and scoring, but has been repeatedly demonstrated to be highly sensitive for the diagnosis of brain impairment when used by trained and experienced clinicians (Reed, Reitan, & Klove, 1965; Reitan, 1971; Selz & Reitan, 1979). Because of the complexities of both administration and scoring, as well as the time involved, the Reitan Children's Batteries have traditionally been used by clinicans with a background in brain-behavior relationships who believe that whether or not a child suffers brain impairment is a significant question deserving the time commitment necessary for valid use of the Batteries.

It is probably safe to say that, in the hands of experienced clinicans, either the Luria or Reitan Test Batteries can result in valid conclusions concerning a child's neuropsychological status: the finding of 91% agreement (Berg et al, 1984) between the two batteries provides limited support for this conclusion. Each battery provides a comprehensive assessment of major abilities necessary for the formulation of a valid diagnosis, and the standardized nature of each battery helps insure that nothing of consequence is likely to be overlooked by the skilled user. Further, the standardized administration format and scoring can be helpful in the generation of a research and clinical data base, because the same measures will be available for all children evaluated. Both batteries, though providing helpful data in formulating an individualized education program (IEP), tend to involve measures which do not by themselves meet the requirements of many school systems. Thus diagnosticians in these settings may use the neuropsychological battery as a supplement to more conventional measures.

In addition to using the standard neuropsychological batteries described above, some school diagnosticians have derived neuro-psychological information from conventional psychoeducational evaluations. An example of this approach utilizes a fairly traditional psychoeducational battery which is augmented by a careful developmental history, behavioral observations during testing, and two simple tests of motor function and one sensory-perceptual measure. This approach has been reported to be adequate for both psychoeducational and neuropsychological evaluation, as well as for developing optimum intervention strategies (e.g., Hartlage, 1975, 1979, 1981, 1982, 1984b; Hartlage & Hartlage, 1982; Hartlage & Reynolds, 1981; Hartlage & Telzrow, 1982, 1983, 1984). This battery uses the age-appropriate Wechsler scale; measures of achievement (e.g., Wide Range Achievement Test); receptive language (e.g., Peabody Picture Vocabulary Test-Revised); constructional praxis (e.g., Beery Developmental Test of Visual-Motor Integration or Bender Motor Gestalt Test), two simple motor measures involving grip strength and finger tapping; and a sensory-perceptual measure involving recognition of numbers written on fingertips. Developmental history focuses on the ages at which the child reached given language and nonlanguage milestones (e.g., Hartlage & Lucas, 1973), whereas behavioral observations during testing focus on compulsive vs. careless general behaviors and specific reactions to given items on which the child experiences difficulty.

The advantages of such an approach include the use of instruments with which most educational diagnosticians are familiar, and which meet requirements of most school systems for the development of an IEP. Although not designed as a neuropsychological battery, these measures provide data on the efficiency of most cortical areas relevant for educational diagnosis and planning, with grossly proportional representation of functions considered to be mediated by each cerebral hemisphere and bilaterally. The developmental history helps place in context the findings from the psychometric measures. It also provides important clues concerning whether any dysfunction related to neuropsychological substrates more likely represents a chronic condition (e.g., cerebral asymmetry) or an acquired insult (e.g., head trauma). The behavioral observations concerning how the child reacts to frustration on given test items, though providing an additional, if indirect, clue concerning the chronic vs. acquired nature of any dysfunction (e.g., Hartlage, 1982b), can also be useful in developing alternative educational programs. This battery has the advantage of ordinal to interval scaling, with potential for detecting subtle changes, but does not provide measures of more fluid aspects of cognitive function. Sophisticated clinicians with a background in brain-behavior relationships can make neuropsychological diagnostic formulations based on the data from such a battery.

IMPLICATIONS FOR SPECIAL SCHOOL SERVICES

The focus on assessment in neuropsychological evaluation should not be viewed as a debate concerning the relative value of a given neuropsychological battery; as Reynolds (1982) has pointed out, far from being a set of techniques, the major contribution of neuropsychology to educational assessment is the provision of a strong paradigm from which to view test data. There are two major conceptual approaches toward the interpretation of neuropsychological findings for intervention purposes. The approach with the longest history proposes that findings be used to translate deficits in neuropsychological function into remedial strategies. These strategies have variously taken the forms of neurological reorganization (e.g., Delacato, 1959, 1963, 1966); psycholinguistic training (e.g., Minskoff, Wiseman, & Minskoff, 1972); and perceptual training (e.g., Frostig, 1963; Kephart, 1971). Reviews of these deficit-remediation strategies have consistently found little evidence for their efficacy (e.g., Goodman and Hammill, 1973; Larsen, 1974; Held, 1965; Sabatino, Miller, & Schmidt, 1981; Wiederholt & Hammill, 1971), but some psychologists continue to recommend attention to deficit areas (e.g., Gordon, 1984). From a theoretical perspective, the notion of teaching to dysfunctional brain tissue has its origins in the equipotentiality theories of Lashley which are contradicted by more recent discoveries (e.g., Bogin, 1975; Chi, Dooling, & Gilles, 1977; Gazzaniga, 1974; Geschwind & Levitsky, 1968; Kinsbourne & Hiscock, 1978).

More contemporary strategies, involving a strength model of educational planning, cite research in neuropsychology and genetics to suggest that deficit models of intervention are doomed to failure (e.g., Hartlage & Reynolds, 1981; Reynolds, 1981; Zarske, 1982). Such strength-oriented intervention strategies are growing in popularity (Gutkin, 1980) and have demonstrated positive outcomes (e.g., Hartlage, 1984c; Hartlage & Reynolds, 1981; Kaufman,

1979). Perhaps one reason for the apparent success of the strength model involves the fact that the child is reinforced for accomplishment, rather than exposed to continued failure and frustration (Blackman, Bilsky, Burger & Mar, 1976; Das, Leong, & Williams, 1978; Doehring, 1968; Krwyaniuk, 1974). To a considerable extent, the strength model is like an extension of the pedagogical principles inherent in Cronbach's (1975) aptitude-treatment interaction, whereby optimum treatment programs for children are based on each child's unique characteristics (Kaufman & Kaufman, 1983).

CONCLUSION

Most knowledge in neuropsychology has been generated within the past two decades. Hence, there is still considerable need for basic research concerning the types of data about brain functioning which are most useful in planning educational services for special children. Those strategies which use the accumulated knowledge of neurological science as the basis for translating findings into interventions (e.g., Hartlage & Hartlage, 1982) appear to offer most promise, although as Reynolds (1982) has pointed out, relatively few individuals are qualified to do so at this time. As interest in applying neuropsychology to school practice begins to be reflected in the content of graduate school programs, this personnel shortage is likely to abate. Present trends suggest that the next decade will witness greater incorporation of brain-behavior paradigms into educational thinking, hopefully with the result that special services providers will have additional tools to meet the needs of exceptional children.

REFERENCES

Berg, R.A., Bolter, J.F., Ch'ien, L.O., Williams, S.J., Lancaster, W. & Cummings, J. (1984). Comparative Diagnostic Accuracy of the Halstead-Reitan and Luria Nebraska Neuropsychological Adult and Childrens Batteries. *International Journal of Clinical Neuropsychology*, 7, 200–204.

Blackman, L.S., Bilsky, L.H., Berger, A.L., & Mar, H. (1976). Cognitive processes and academic achievement in EMR adolescents. *American Journal of Mental Deficiency*, 81, 125–134.

Bogin, J. (1975). Some educational aspects of hemispheric specialization, *UCLA Educator*, 24–32.

Bonivillion, J.D., Nelson, K.E., & Ryne, J.M. (1981). Sign language and autism. *Journal of Autism and Developmental Disorders, 11*, 125–137.

Broca, P. (1863). Localisation des fonctions cerebrales: siege du language articule. *Bulletin Societe Anthropolgie, 4*, 200–204.

Chi, J.G., Dooling, E.C., & Gilles, F.H. (1977). Left-right asymmetries of the temporal speech area of the human fetus. *Archives of Neurology, 34*, 346–348.

Cronbach, L.J. (1975). Beyond two disciplines of scientific psychology. *American Psychologist, 30*, 116–127.

Das, J.P., Leong, C.K., & Williams, N.H. (1978). The relationship between learning disability & simultaneous successive processing. *Journal of Learning Disabilities, 11*, 618–625.

Delecato, C.H. (1959). *The Treatment and Prevention of reading problems: The Neuropsychological approach.* Springfield, IL: Charles C. Thomas.

Delecato, C.H. (1963). *The Diagnosis and treatment of speech and reading problems.* Springfield, IL: Charles C. Thomas.

Delecato, C.H. (1966). *Neurological organization and reading.* Springfield, IL: Charles C. Thomas.

Doehring, D.G. (1968). *Patterns of impairment in specific reading disabilities.* Bloomington, Indiana: University Press.

Frostig, M. (1963). *Frostig developmental test of visual perception.* Palo Alto, CA: Consulting Psychologists Press.

Galaburda, A.M., LeMay, M., Keeper, T.L., & Geschwind, N. (1978). Right-left assymmetries in the brain. *Science, 199*, 852–856.

Gazzaniga, M. (1974). Cerebral dominance viewed as a decision system. In S. Dimons & J. Beaumont (Eds), *Hemispheric functions in the human brain.* London: Halstead Press.

Geary, D.C., Jennings, S.M., Schultz, D.D., & Alper, J.G. (1984). The diagnostic accuracy of the Luria-Nebraska Neuropsychological battery-children's revision for 9–12 year learning disabled children. *School Psychology Review, 13*, 375–380.

Geschwind, N. & Levitsky, W. (1968). Human Brain: Left-right asymetries in temporal speech areas. *Science, 161*, 186–187.

Golden, C.J. (1981). A standardized version of Luria's neuropsychological tests: A quantitative and qualitative approach to neuropsychological evaluation. In S. Filskov & T. Boll (Eds), *Handbook of Clinical Neuropsychology* (pp. 608–642). New York: Wiley.

Golden, C.J. (1981). The Luria-Nebraska Children's battery: Theory and formulation. In Hynd, G.W. & Obrzut, J.E. (Eds.) *Neuropsychological assessment and the school-age child: New issues and procedures.* New York: Grune & Stratton.

Golden, C.J., Kane, R., Sweet, J., Moses, J.A., Cardellino, J.P., Templeton, R., Vicente, P., & Graber, B. (1981). Relationship of the Halstead-Reitan Neuropsychological Battery to the Luria-Nebraska Neuropsychological Battery. *Journal of Consulting and Clinical Psychology, 19*, 410–417.

Goodman, L., & Hammill, D. (1973). The effectiveness of Kephart-Hetman activities in developing perceptual-motor and cognitive skills. *Focus on Exceptional Children. 4*, 1–9.

Gordon, H.W. (1984). Dyslexia. In R. Tarter & G. Goldstien (Eds.), *Advances in clinical neuropsychology* (pp. 181–205). New York: Plenum.

Gutkin, T.B. (1980). Teacher perceptions of consultation services provided by school psychologists. *Professional Psychology, 11*, 637–642.

Hammill, D.D., & Larsen, S.C. (1974). The effectiveness of psycholinguistic training. *Exceptional children, 41*, 5–14.

Hartlage, L.C. (1975). Neuropsychological approaches to predicting outcome of remedial educational strategies for learning disabled children. *Pediatric Psychology, 3*, 23.

Hartlage, L.C. (1979). Management of common clinical problems: Learning disabilities. *School Related Health Care* (Ross Laboratories monograph #9), 28–33.

Hartlage, L.C. (1981). Clinical application of neuropsychological data. *School Psychology Review, 10*, 362–366.

Hartlage, L.C. (1982). Neuropsychological Assessment Techniques. In C. Reynolds & T. Gutkin (Eds.) *Handbook of School Psychology*, (p. 296–318). New York: Wiley.

Hartlage, L.C. (1982b). *Neuropsychological evaluation of learning and behavior problems in children*. American Psychological Association Continuing Education Workshop, Washington, D.C.

Hartlage, L.C. (1984a, April). *The use of neuropsychological assessment procedures by school psychologists*. Paper presented at National Association of School Psychologists, Philadelphia.

Hartlage, L.C. (1984b). Neuropsychological Assessment of Children. In P.A. Keller (Ed.) *Innovations in Clinical Practice, 3,* 153–165.

Hartlage, L.C. (1984c, October). *Neuropsychological approaches to enhancing learning in individuals of superior ability*. Paper presented at National Academy of Neuropsychologists, San Diego.

Hartlage, L.C., Hartlage, P.L. (1982). Psychological evaluation in neurological disease. In J. Youmans (Eds.), *Neurological Surgery*, pp. 701–716, New York: W.B. Saunders.

Hartlage, L.C., Lucas, D.G. (1973). *Mental Development Evaluation of the Pediatric Patient*. Springfield, IL: Charles C. Thomas.

Hartlage, L.C., Reynolds, C.R. (1981). Individual educational programs (IEP's) and neuropsychological differentiation. In G. Hynd & J. Obrzut (Eds.), *Neuropsychological Assessment and the School Age Child: Issues and Procedures*. New York: Grune & Stratton.

Hartlage, L.C., Telzrow, C.F. (1982). Specific preschool medical findings which predict specific learning outcomes. In W. Cruickshank and J. Lerner (Eds.), *Best of ACLD*. Syracuse: Syracuse University Press.

Hartlage, L.C., Telzrow, C.F. (1983). The Neuropsychological basis of educational intervention. *Journal of Learning Disabilities, 16,* 521–528.

Hartlage, L.C., Telzrow, C.F. (1984). Rehabilitation of persons with learning disabilities, *Journal of Rehabilitation, 50,* 31–34.

Hartlage, L.C., Telzrow, C.F. (1983). Assessment of Neurological Functioning. In K. Paget & B. Bracken (Eds.), *Psychoeducational Assessment of Preschool and Primary Aged Children*, New York: Grune & Stratton.

Hauser, S.L., DeLong, G.R., & Rosman, N.P. (1975). Pneumographic findings in the infantile autism syndrome. *Brain, 98,* 667–688.

Kanner, L. (1943). Autistic disturbances of affective contact. *Nervous Child, 2,* 217–250.

Kaufman, A.S. (1979). *Intelligent testing with the WISC-R*. New York: Wiley-Interscience.

Kaufman, N.L. & Kaufman, A.S. (1983). Remedial intervention in education. In G.W. Hynd (Ed.), *The school psychologist: Contemporary perspective*. Syracuse: Syracuse University Press.

Kephart, N. (1971). *The slow learner in the class room* (rev. ed.) Columbus, OH: Charles E. Merril.

Kinsbourne, M., & Hiscock, M. (1978). Cerebral lateralization and cognitive development. In J. Chall & Musky (Eds.), *Education and the Brain*: Seventy-seventh yearbook for the national society for the study of education. Chicago: University of Chicago Press.

Krwyaniuk, L.W. (1974). Patterns of cognitive abilities of high and low achieving school children. Unpublished doctoral dissertation, University of Alberta, Alberta, Canada.

Minskoff, E., Wiseman, D.E., & Minskoff, G.G. (1972). *The MWM program for developing language abilities*. Ridgefield, N.J: Educational Performance.

Moses, J.A. & Golden, C.J. (1979). The discriminative effectiveness of the standardized neuropsychological battery. *International Journal of Neuroscience, 9,* 149–155.

Orton, S.T. (1928). Specific reading disability-strephosymbolia. *Journal of the American Medical Association, 90,* 1095.

Orton, S.T. (1937). *Reading, Writing and Speech problems in children*. New York: Norton.

Reed, H.B.C., Reitan, R.M., Klove, H. (1965). Influence of cerebral lesions on psychological test performances of older children. *Journal of Consulting Psychology*, 29, 247–251.

Reitan, R.M. (1971). Sensorimotor functions in brain-damaged and normal children of early school age. *Perceptual and Motor Skills, 33*, 655–664.

Reynolds, C.R. (1981). The Neuropsychological basis of intelligence. In G.W. Hynd & J.E. Obrzut (Eds.), *Neuropsychological Assessment and the School-Aged Child.* New York: Grune & Stratton.

Reynolds, C.R. (1982). Neuropsychological assessment in education: A caution. *Journal of Research and Development in Education, 15*, 76–79.

Sabatino, D.A., Miller, T.L., & Schmidt, C. (1981). *Learning Disabilities* MD: Aspen Systems Corp.

Selz, M. (1981). Halstead-Reitan neuropsychological test batteries for children. In G.W. Hynd, & J.E. Obrzut, (Eds.), *Neuropsychological assessment procedures,* New York: Grune & Stratton.

Selz, M. & Reitan, R.M. (1979). Rules for neuropsychological diagnosis: Classification of brain function in older children. *Journal of Consulting and Clinical Psychology, 47*, 258–264.

Semmes, J. (1968). Hemispheric specialization: a possible clue to mechanism. *Neuropsychologia, 6*, 11–26.

Smith, A. (1966). Certain hypothesized hemispheric differences in language and visual functions in human adults. *Cortex, 2*, 109–126.

Warrington, E.K., James, M. & Kinsbourne, M. (1966). Drawing disability in relation to laterality of cerebral lesion. *Brain, 86*, 53–82.

Webster, J.S. & Dostrau, V. (1982). Efficacy of a decision-tree approach to the Luria-Nebraska Neuropsychological Battery. *Journal of Consulting & Clinical Psychology, 50*, 313–315.

Webster, J.S., Dostrau, V. & Scott, R.R. (1983). A decision-tree approach to the Luria-Nebraska Neuropsychological Battery, *International Journal of Clinical Neuropsychology, 6*, 17–21.

Wernicke, K. (1874). *Das Aphasische Symptomekomplex.* Brestan: Cohn & Neigart.

Wiederholt, J.L., & Hammill, D.D. (1971). Use of Frostig-Horne perception program in the urban school. *Psychology in the Schools, 8*, 268–274.

Wilkening, G.N. (1981). The Luria-Nebraska Neuropsychological Battery-Children's Revision: A preliminary report. Paper presented at the 89th Annual Meeting of the American Psychological Association. Los Angeles, CA.

Zarske, J.A. (1982). Neuropsychological intervention approaches for handicapped children. *Journal of Research and Development in Education, 15*, 66–75.

Personality Assessment and Children: A Critical Appraisal and Emerging Trends

David W. Barnett

University of Cincinnati

ABSTRACT. An analysis of the criticisms of children's personality assessment and a discussion of emerging trends are offered in this review. A distinction is made between the assessment of personal and social functioning, implicit in all educational decisions, and the use of personality tests and techniques. It is noted that personality research has not been directly concerned with the professional practice issues inherent in children's personality assessment. Finally, guidelines for personality assessment are offered.

Many may be surprised by a discussion of personality in a review of assessment developments for exceptional children. The topic is controversial and recently has been neglected or severely criticized in major sources (Salvia & Ysseldyke, 1981). However, there has been a widespread resurgence of interest in personality assessment and its future is important.

An analysis of the criticisms of personality assessment is presented, followed by a discussion of emerging trends. Guidelines for personality assessment are offered, but they address only some of the practical and conceptual limitations associated with this assessment activity. Although factors related to personal and social functioning are a part of all educational decisions and need to be addressed, personality assessment techniques should be critically evaluated as a part of problem solving procedures. New methods are required in order to incorporate research developments into practice.

Appreciation is expressed to Karl B. Zucker who helped in the formulation of many ideas contained in the paper through numerous discussions.

Requests for reprints should be sent to: David W. Barnett, College of Education, University of Cincinnati, Mail Location #2, Cincinnati, OH 45221.

CRITICISMS OF PERSONALITY ASSESSMENT

The "demise" of personality assessment can be related to several factors (Cleveland, 1976). First, the field has been plagued by pervasive measurement problems. Personality tests simply have not predicted behavior very well (Mischel, 1968), at least not to the degree required by professional practice decisions. A closer look at the measurement issues is in order.

Personality tests have such diverse origins, that, at first glance, it may appear that personality assessment lacks any "representative" viewpoint at all. Major theorists disagree on the dimensions and organization of personality, and the measurement of personality processes. The field may be characterized by its "cultures," although there is evidence for rapprochement as well (Korchin & Schuldberg, 1981).

Available techniques may be built upon a theory of personality, psychopathology, logical and/or statistical relationships between items and behaviors, or no well-defined approach at all. New tests may be based upon older theories. Most research underlying personality assessment is concerned with the study of adult personality. Therefore, developmental issues and constructs important to children (e.g., play) may be ignored. The manner in which tests are constructed and used can result in pessimistic outcomes for children. The entire process is abused if possibilities for change implicit in development are neglected by the assessment procedures and decisions (Brim & Kagan, 1980; Messick, 1983). Because of the problems encountered, a number of ethical and humanistic concerns have been raised (e.g., Sugarman, 1978).

A second related criticism pertains to levels of inference and "clinical judgment" required by interpretations of test responses and other behaviors. Many psychologists are uncomfortable about the almost mystical quality of projective test interpretation, but the issue is not directly resolved through the use of "objective" procedures. The personality assessor is guided in test selection and interpretation by the work of the test author, and by formal or informal "personal" theories, each having a potentially unknown degree of influence. Actual decision-making processes are not founded on research and are difficult to study or replicate. Practitioners often seem to ignore research findings related to personality assessment practices (Wade & Baker, 1977). Theories cannot be adequately tested, including either those of the test author or those of the psychologist.

A third criticism pertains to the practical uses of personality assessment. Assessment procedures have been studied with respect to classification, description, and prediction. Although these different emphases are important, they are often of only limited value to practitioners. For example, when faced with a classification decision (e.g., Is the child emotionally disturbed?), reliable behaviors will be sought to the possible exclusion of variables associated with helping. Even though research supports certain behavioral syndromes (Achenbach & Edelbrock, 1978), major problems are evident in classification systems (Garber, 1984). Personality tests will not provide a direct answer to diagnostic questions posed by the classification systems used in DSM III (the latest diagnostic system of the American Psychiatric Association) or PL 94-142 (e.g., Rapoport & Ismond, 1984).

The differences implied by the terms "emotionally disturbed," "behavior disordered," and "socially maladjusted," for example, arise in part from assumptions about the nature and origins of psychopathology. Professionals guided by theories that stress either internal attributions concerning behavior (those within the child) or external causes (those attributable to environmental factors) are likely to choose different assessment techniques and treatment alternatives. However, such distinctions are superficial and both need to be taken into account. Phillips, Draguns, and Bartlett (1975) stress that classification systems should be open to change, tied to developmental research, and responsive to unintended negative outcomes. Future classification systems also are likely to be descriptive of the types of services needed by the child, thus the assessment of the service delivery *system* would be required.

If the purpose of personality assessment is increased understanding, its techniques may yield information about the possible manner in which personality is structured (Dielman & Barton, 1983) though little information directly concerning the processes involved in helping the child adapt to specific circumstances may result. The outcomes related to personality description are likely to vary widely by the method and rater selected.

Many psychologists view prediction (e.g., future adjustment, need for intervention, likelihood of success in a treatment program) as the major goal in personal and social measurement. The utility of personality assessment techniques for long range forecasts or for the design of children's interventions has not been demonstrated. It is important to note that the criticisms are not indictments of personality research. Much of value has been learned about factors related to personal and social functioning, and continued research in the above areas is essential. The results should be judged in part by the extremely complex nature of the goals that have been outlined above and the different objectives of research and professional practice.

ALTERNATIVES TO PERSONALITY ASSESSMENT

Many professionals have tried to circumvent problems associated with personality assessment in ways that still allow complex thinking about children. The major attempts are encompassed by eclectic, atheoretical and behavioral approaches. Eclectisism, the most prevalent model (e.g., Garfield & Kurtz, 1977), draws from diverse sources. Although this has softened disputes (Weiner, 1983), personal eclecticism is not systematic. Each professional is guided by different, often unspecified, assumptions regarding behavior.

Lanyon and Goodstein (1982) use an atheoretical definition: personality refers to "enduring characteristics of the person which are significant for his/her interpersonal behavior" (p. 43). Personality assessment is "the process of gathering and organizing information about another person in the expectation that this information will lead to a better understanding of the person" (Lanyon & Goodstein, 1982, p. 39). However, even though formal theories may not define personality assessment procedures and their interpretation, informal ones do. The process results in eclecticism, with little reason to expect agreement across psychologists.

Behaviorists have been among the most vocal critics of traditional personality assessment (Goldfried & Kent, 1972). In general, a problem solving model is stressed by behaviorists (D'Zurilla & Goldfried, 1971), as are direct measures of coping or adjustment. In designing an intervention, socially significant behaviors and contexts, both assumed to be potentially modifiable, are assessed (Kanfer & Saslow, 1969). Further, the client relationship is planned as "an apprenticeship in problem solving" (Mahoney, 1974, p. 274). However, contemporary behaviorists employ "person" variables, especially self-regulatory, phenomenological (individualistic), and symbolic processes. Many of the measurement difficulties associated with more traditional approaches remain unresolved (Kendall & Hollon, 1981; Roberts & Nelson, 1984).

RATIONALE FOR PERSONALITY ASSESSMENT

Given the widespread criticisms and potential abuses, what rationale for personality assessment can exist? The answer is not straightforward. The strongest argument is that factors related to personality assessment are implicit in all educational decisions and programs (Barnett, 1983). The purpose and methods are clearer for emotionally disturbed/behavior disordered children but have broader applicability. When concerned about the effects of a handicapping condition, special class placement or other intervention, professionals and parents are ultimately concerned not only about the acquisition of specific skills related to educational, social or vocational gains, but with more important and less tangible issues related to life adjustment.

Special education teachers face complex problems that cut across arbitrary boundaries of exceptionality and deal with facets of personality every day in some manner (e.g., self-concept, others-concept). Personality variables are important to the study of behaviors (agression, social skills, adaptive behavior, coping). The effects of stress (e.g., Rutter, 1981) brought about by handicaps and other conditions are mediated by personality variables.

Personality assessment is integrative: it requires the simultaneous consideration of subjective experiences, personal goals, skills, and motivations of the child and significant others. Personality assessment is concerned with issues related to development, adaptation, and coping over long time periods. In contrast to other assessment approaches (e.g., educational, behavioral), the goal is a relatively complete view of the child central to the study of adjustment. Emerging models of personality assessment include parents, teachers, and children in both assessment and intervention.

Is personality assessment practical? In a traditional sense, the answer is no. The potential benefits are equal to the skills of the assessor. However, because personal and social adjustment is a part of every psychoeducational assessment, better methods are needed to take such factors into account.

EMERGING TRENDS IN PERSONALITY THEORY, RESEARCH, AND ASSESSMENT PRACTICE

Reconceptualization of Trait Approaches

Psychologists agree on the existence or importance of personality (Allport, 1937; Stagner, 1984). There is significant disagreement, however, on how to study personality and the current usefulness of doing so. Much of the controversy involving personality assessment has centered on the status, meaning and measurement of *traits*.

Early and continued use of the term suggests to some an overly rigid, "fundamental" framework for studying individuals based in neuropsychic structure and developmental experiences. Much research associated with the trait approach has ambitiously sought "basic units of personality" that would demonstrate "widely generalized causal effects on behavior" (Mischel, 1973, p. 253). However, trait approaches have been reconceptualized by many authors.

For example, Stagner (1984) defines trait as "a consistent and persistent pattern of behavior and experience (cognitive and affective) characteristic of a particular individual" (p. 7). Hogan, DeSoto, and Solano (1977) argue that most theorists *use* "trait" to refer to "stylistic consistencies in interpersonal behavior" and not to "theoretical primitives" supposedly measured by tests (p. 256). Researchers do not generally believe that traits are necessarily "enduring psychic structures" (p. 257).

Psychological tests have been developed as an *economical* tool to determine important "general characteristics" (Peterson, 1968), but the value of constructing instruments to measure these characteristics may be limited, apart from research and theory. Major scales take years and countless funds to develop, and, depending on the purpose for which they were developed, they may neglect important issues in the search for common features of personality (e.g., Burisch, 1984).

Mischel (1968, 1973) has questioned the usefulness of trait-like approaches to personality measurement. While evidence for predictability can be found in cognitive behaviors, for example, and for samples of behavior across similar situations, complex social behaviors are less well related to the "traits" measured by personality tests. Others have pointed out, however, that sound measures of personality are predictive of important behaviors (Hogan,

DeSoto, & Solano, 1977); Stagner, 1984). Researchers have been able to increase correlations substantially from those typically found in personality studies, thus lending support to the consistency of traits (e.g., Epstein, 1984). Substantial evidence exists for continuity of personality development over long time periods (Block & Block, 1980).

Still the practical utility of trait-like approaches to personality assessment needs to be demonstrated, especially for children. The same correlations that provide some support for the continuity of development and the predictive validity of various tests also suggest considerable error for individuals. The variables associated with change are not taken into account. Mischel (1984) emphasizes that the study of person variables should be linked to basic psychological processes and situations.

Contributions of Ecological, Psychosocial, and Cognitive Behavioral Assessment

Though personality assessment has not been tied to the development of helping strategies for children, other types of assessment have evolved which are directly concerned with this goal. Although overlapping, assessment systems necessary for planning and interpreting the results of treatment-oriented personality assessment are depicted in Figure 1.

The ecological approach requires a broad study of the social and physical environments of the child (Brubakken, Derouin, & Morrison, 1980; Hobbs, 1979). Assessment procedures focus on the determination of relevant systems and persons (Hartman, 1978) and should include multiple viewpoints. Consideration should be given to the quality of personal and social learning experiences. The goal is not necessarily "cure"; rather, the problem is defined as "doing what we can to make a small social system work in a reasonably satisfactory manner" (Hobbs, 1966, p. 1108).

Psychosocial and psychosituational assessment stress the importance of skills necessary across settings and those needed for adaptation to specific settings, respectively. Social skills assessment and training is an example of the emphasis on cross-situational behaviors (Ladd & Mize, 1983; Michelson, Sugai, Wood, & Kazdin, 1983). Psychosituational assessment illustrates an in-depth analysis of adaptation to specific settings (e.g., Ellett & Bersoff,

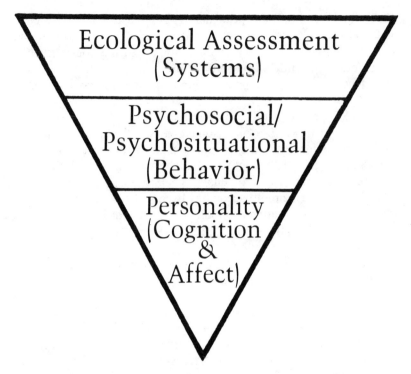

FIGURE 1. Systems of assessment necessary for planning and interpreting treat-ment-oriented personality assessment.

1976). Behaviors, and expectations of the referral agent in relation-ship to the child, are analyzed.

The cognitive behavioral trend has given renewed sanction to the study of private phenomena and the subjective experience. It includes the functional analysis of the client's thinking processes, inventory of cognitive skills, and imaginal and fantasy experiences as they apply to personal adjustment and social behavior (Kendall & Hollon, 1981; Meichenbaum, 1977). Mahoney (1974) reminds us that most behavior is private, thus not directly observable. Recently the "unconscious" has been considered from the perspective of developments in the behavioral sciences. Cognitive events and conscious experiences have links, although they may not be "obvious or direct," to unconscious processes (Meichenbaum & Bowers, 1984, p. 4). They may be highly significant for cognitive behavioral assessments—"a reversal of the original behavioral point of view" (Meichenbaum & Gilmore, 1984, p. 290).

Reciprocal Determinism: The Unit of Analysis in Personality Assessment

Bandura (1977a) has been central in developing the social learning perspective from which diverse theoretical and practical applications have emanated. Social learning stresses "reciprocal-determinism" as the basic principle for the study of complex behavior. Reciprocal determinism addresses the long standing debate as to the relative significance of personality, behavior, and situations. "Behavior, internal personal factors, and environmental influences all operate as interlocking determinants of each other" (Bandura, 1978, p. 346).

Assessments of persons: A social learning analysis. Rather than "broad dimensions," "basic factors," "pervasive motives," or "traits" for understanding adjustment, the stress should be on the unique organization of the behavior within the individual (Mischel, 1973). Key behaviors that tend to define attributes of interest should be assessed, not all behaviors that may have a superficial resemblance (Mischel, 1984). Mischel (1973, 1981) suggests the following "person" variables allowing for the study of interactions between affect, thought or cognition, overt behaviors and situations:

1. *Cognitive and behavioral competencies* refer to the individual's potential "to construct (generate) diverse behaviors under appropriate conditions" (1973, p. 265). They result from cognitive and social development, and from knowledge of the rules that determine behavior.
2. *Encoding strategies and constructs* stress the phenomenological manner, or the personal constructs, that people use to "perceive, think, interpret, and experience the world" (1981, p. 486).
3. *Personal and subjective expectancies* bridge the gap between what people are able to do and how they actually perform. Relatively specific (and modifiable) subjective hypotheses about behavior-outcome contingencies and personal competencies are assessed.
4. *Subjective values and preferences* focus attention on "behaviors people choose to perform" and the functions of various incentives (1981, p. 490). It is important to assess "major stimuli that have . . . the power to induce positive or negative emotional states" (1981, p. 490).

5. *Self-regulatory systems and plans* suggest a careful analysis of self-adopted "goals and standards" (1981, p 491).

Other Major Assessment Trends

With adults, it is more tenable to assess a broader repertoire and more stable patterns of behavior, and skills that may have been lost or never developed. In contrast, children's personality assessment should focus on learning contexts, learning processes, and emerging skills. The last has received the least amount of attention, and signifies the clearest break with tradition. Emerging skills include, for example, socially appropriate behaviors that are (a) in the formative stages, (b) rare or intermittent, or (c) only elicited during naturally occurring environmental changes or behavioral interventions. In order to adequately assess competencies, predict possibilities for future adaptation, and plan interventions, optimal performances need to be assessed (e.g., Mischel, 1981).

The recent trends reflect the complexity of behavior, and the corresponding need for "multiple goals for measurement" (Mischel, 1977): "If . . . behavior is determined by many interacting [personal and environmental] variables . . . then a focus on any one of them is likely to lead to limited predictions and generalizations" (p. 246). Specific, multiple, and continuous assessment targets are central to the study of adjustment and the design of interventions (Barlow, Hayes, & Nelson, 1984). New techniques are needed that are based on different assessment functions (Hawkins, 1979).

CHILDREN'S PERSONALITY ASSESSMENT: GUIDELINES FOR SCHOOL PRACTITIONERS

What is Personality Assessment?

Lacking consensus in personality theory (e.g., Hall & Lindzey, 1978), one should not expect agreement in defining personality assessment (Lanyon & Goodstein, 1982). Personality assessment is perhaps best defined by its different functions, but namely, researchers have been interested in traits, the organization and structure of personality, and the prediction of socially significant behaviors (Wiggins, 1973). Professional psychologists have been interested in the helping role. Personality assessment defined by the latter function is different from the other conceptualizations in several ways. First, an attempt is made to identify significant, covert or internal personality processes important in the planning of interventions; those that, at least in part, are externally verifiable. Second, personality constructs that have at least some reasonable amount of validity for the client are used to guide assessments. Third, personality tests are evaluated on a case-by-case basis for their potential usefulness. Fourth, findings are interpreted through the use of a contemporary theoretical framework. However, in contrast to a theory of personality or psychopathology, the theory used is more typically related to psychosocial change.

The Use of Constructs Related to Psychosocial Change

Constructs that stem from research in psychosocial change are used to guide assessments, interpret findings, and to design interventions. First, person and situation variables are described in an *idiographic* manner. This term (Allport, 1937; Runyan, 1983) defines indepth individual analysis, in contrast to the identification of general laws. The phenomenological (subjective) impact of situations and behaviors of concern is studied from the viewpoint of the client and significant others without preconceived ideas about what behaviors should be addressed or how (e.g., Kendall & Hollon, 1981; Mischel, 1984).

Second, child, family and community systems are screened, not only for adjustment problems, but also for strengths such as healthy, adaptive mechanisms and coping strategies. One screening method is to identify naturally occurring approximations to successful strategies that can be expanded through training experiences. Interviews may reveal that caregivers have a rudimentary grasp or partial sets of skills but are not aware of the value and logical extensions of their behaviors. Examples for personal and social development include: (a) encouraging social maturity, (b) modeling problem-solving skills, (c) avoiding physical and mental punishment, and (d) increasing appropriate parental responsivity. In addition to psychological and social processes that create and maintain temporary behaviors, environments that provide mediated (structured) learning experiences over relatively long time periods are subject to analysis (Hobbs, 1979; Laosa & Sigel, 1982). Thus, an evaluation of satisfaction and support in relationships between child and caregivers, and community, is important (Werner, 1982).

Third, the results of the idiographic assessment and ecological assessment are used to define appropriate behaviors for further assessment. Negative, bizarre, or unusual behaviors can often be recast through an analysis of specific cognitive and/or social behaviors that are prerequisite to desired objectives. The maladaptive behaviors are explored in terms of barriers to adjustment; confirming as well as disconfirming evidence of problems is evaluated.

Fourth, other person and situational variables based on research are assessed. This step includes a systematic review of treatment options available and the magnitude or clinical significance of reported change based upon validated interventions and/or replicated case studies. Child and setting characteristics, intervention components and loci (Glenwick & Jason, 1984), observational systems and/or dependent variables are all points of analysis. ·

Beliefs about the modifiability of the behaviors are assessed from the perspectives of the relevant persons. Central are the client's beliefs about change. Bandura (1977b, 1981) has proposed *self-efficacy* as a broadly integrative developmental construct. Self-efficacy relates to personal beliefs about competency: "judgments about how well one can organize and execute courses of action required to deal with prospective situations that may contain ambiguous, unpredictable, and often stressful elements" (1981, p. 200–201). Perceived self-efficacy has the potential for influencing the child's, parents' and teacher's choice of activities and persistence in solving difficult tasks. "Those who persist in subjectively-threatening activities that are in fact relatively safe will gain corrective experiences that reinforce their sense of efficacy. . . . Those who cease their coping efforts prematurely will retain their self-debilitating expectations and fears for a long time" (1977b, p. 194).

The Use of Methods in Personality Assessment

Professionals cannot rely on any specific technology, test, or test battery. Each should be considered as potential sources of information and hypotheses and as potential sources of error (Barnett & Zucker, 1985).

Sources of information and hypotheses. Methods for assessing personality include nontest-based tools (interviews, observations), and more formally derived techniques (rating scales, objective tests, projectives). Each of these methods may be used to evaluate adaptation, barriers to adjustment, and personality processes.

Nontest-based techniques such as interviews and observations enable gathering of information unlikely to be obtained from tests. Interviews, while not treated as formally as other assessment methods (Gresham, 1984), provide a mechanism for problem identification and clarification through an examination of consistencies and contrasts of the problem as perceived by parents, teachers, child, and others. The interview steps range from a "scanning operation" to an "extended inquiry." Although problem oriented, decisions may be made to broaden the scope of the interview to help evaluate (a) facets of psychological constructs and personality variables (e.g., motivation, depression, anxiety), (b) family history, structure, and values, and (c) plans for interventions (Peterson, 1968).

Guidelines for observational techniques have been extensively discussed. As with other methods, observations are important for assessing facets of personality. The findings of a behavioral assessment should be integrated into a comprehensive view of the person. In doing so, it may be necessary to consider (a) levels of personality, (b) self-awareness, and (c) mechanisms of control (Barnett & Zucker, 1985). For example, a child viewed by self and others as nonaggressive may still have violent fantasies. The assessment of covert or private phenomena (thoughts, feelings, sensations) can take place to a degree through self-observation and recording (Roberts & Nelson, 1984), and should be integrated with the results of observational studies.

The defining attribute of test or technique-based assessments is that they are guided by the theory and procedures of the test author or researcher. Rating scales, projectives and objectives are included under this classification in addition to highly structured interview and observational systems. Many rating scales can be thought of as adjuncts to observations and interviews whereby parents, teachers and clients are asked to estimate the presence, absence or extent of behavior, the behaviors of significant others, and aspects of situations.

Traditional personality tests are represented by two reasonably distinct methods: projective techniques and so-called objective tests. Projective techniques are less structured, a frequent distinguishing feature being an intended diversity of possible responses. Although widely criticized, they remain popular (Goh & Fuller, 1983). Many interpretations and uses are invalid; however, projectives can be used for building rapport, for clarifying affect as well as behavior, and for generating (not confirming) hypotheses. Experimentation with projective-like techniques is often consistent with contemporary interests such as interpersonal problem-solving skills.

Objective techniques include those that represent attempts at personality description (Dielman & Barton, 1983), provide estimates of pathology or adjustment (Wirt, Lachar, Klinedinst, & Seat, 1984), or measure a particular dimension of personality (e.g., self-concept). They may be based on self-reports or observations of others. Decisions about the use of objective measures are based on the match between test validity and the problem behavior. Tests, subscales and individual items may aid in problem detection, problem clarification, and the estimation of the severity of a problem. Tests may also broaden the information base about a child where elaboration is necessary.

Sources of error. Assessment errors may be created by instruments, psychologists, and procedures. Each step in personality assessment is limited by theoretical/conceptual issues and implicit "diagnostic styles" (McDermott, 1981) that are used to (a) define the problem, (b) determine the selection of test instruments, their order, and time spent in the assessment process, (c) identify persons interviewed and questions asked, (d) focus attention on certain features of the setting and not on others, (e) interpret the results, (f) explore a range of treatment options, and (g) determine how the plans should be evaluated.

Personality assessment is also limited by the technical adequacy of the procedures used, and the difficulty of the adjustment problem or client's circumstances. While projective techniques have been widely criticized, the term *objective* may be misleading to a degree. The administration of rating scales and objective measures is straightforward, although, similar to other appraisal methods, interpretation is not (e.g., Edelbrock, 1983). Objective techniques and rating scales may satisfy minimal reliability requirements for some functions but critical validity problems may not be resolved. For example, scales frequently have meanings that vary by population, by different levels of obtained scores, and by patterns of scores. Interpretations may be modified substantially by other assessment findings.

Equally serious error sources are those that involve human

inference. Multiple sets of perceptions require analysis: the psychologist's (Weiner, 1983), the child's, and those of others who contribute to the assessment process. The following are illustrative: the tendency to (a) overestimate personal factors and underestimate environmental factors when considering the behavior of others, (b) assume falsely or prematurely that a consensus has been reached, (c) infer from an inadequate or nonrepresentative sample of behavior, (d) attend to unusual, vivid events at the expense of less impressive behaviors or nonoccurrences of behavior, and (e) adjust observations to confirm favorite theories (see Nisbett & Ross, 1980).

As mentioned, errors are prevalent with respect to diagnostic categories. Although procedures exist with respect to increasing the reliability of certain diagnostic decisions, other unintended outcomes need to be evaluated. More reliable diagnostic categories are not necessarily linked to improved services.

Procedural Safeguards, Problem-Solving Models, and Personality Assessment

The problem solving components of children's personality assessment are summarized in Table 1. The most important features are: (a) implementing procedural safeguards by including multiple perspectives, (b) incorporating the results of major assessment trends, and (c) orienting assessment in a manner consistent with research on psychosocial change.

TABLE 1

A Problem Solving Approach to Personality Assessment

1. Idiographic assessment: define the significant person and situational/system variables from the client's viewpoint.
2. Ecological assessment: screen child, family, and community systems.
3. Behavioral assessment: include maladaptive, adaptive, and emerging behaviors of both child and caregivers, and developmental constructs (e.g., play).
4. Change theory: include systematic assessment of treatment options and client's beliefs about change.
5. Personality research: assess the correspondence between personality constructs, traits/personality styles, as described by

the client and those supported by research. Questions about the appropriateness of constructs are a point of assessment. Specific scales or observations of interest may be used or developed.

6. Personality tests and techniques: base assessment on the match between scale and test validity and the problem behavior. Formal assessment devices should be considered if diagnostic questions cannot be answered through the use of other methods (Weiner, 1972).

Unfortunately, while personality assessment should have implications for decisions concerning placement, the design of interventions, and the determination of significant outcomes, established personality assessment tools are inadequate for these functions. Problem solving guidelines *will*, however, allow one to plan and organize assessment. Such guidelines are useful to the extent that they reduce a *wide spectrum* of error and improve outcomes for children. The problem-solving steps enable the clarification of potential factors that influence the assessment/intervention process.

CONCLUSION

There has been an explosion of research in the areas of personal and social development, but this research has not generally been incorporated into the professional practice of personality assessment. Personality research itself is often only tangential to personality assessment (e.g., Ickes, 1984) and does not necessarily deal with problems or objectives of practitioners.

Research is needed to identify and evaluate a "professional practices model" for children. The practices, or component strategies, associated with children's personality assessment should be based on (a) factors that facilitate development, and (b) exemplary problem solving strategies employed by professionals in real life situations (Schön, 1983). The guidelines presented earlier follow from these objectives. Children's personality assessment cannot be based on eclectic or atheoretical reasoning, but should be founded on an appropriate body of research. The future of personality assessment is promising, and will incorporate advances in measurement, neuroscience and computer technology, as well as research in personality development and behavioral change.

REFERENCES

Achenbach, T. M., & Edelbrock, C. S. (1978). The classification of child psychopathology: A review and analysis. *Psychological Bulletin, 85*, 1275–1301.

Allport, G. W. (1937). *Personality: A psychological interpretation.* New York: Holt.

Bandura, A. (1977a). *Social learning theory.* Englewood Cliffs, NJ: Prentice-Hall.

Bandura, A. (1977b). Self-efficacy: Toward a unifying theory of behavior change. *Psychological Review, 84*, 191–215.

Bandura, A. (1978). The self-system in reciprocal determinism *American Psychologist, 33*, 344–358.

Bandura, A. (1981). Self-referent thought: A developmental analysis of self-efficacy. In J. H. Flavell & L. Ross (Eds.), *Social cognitive development: Frontiers and possible futures* (pp. 200–239). New York: Cambridge University Press.

Barlow, D. H., Hayes, S. C., & Nelson, R. O. (1984). *The scientist practitioner: Research and accountability in clinical and educational settings.* New York: Pergamon.

Barnett, D. (1983). *Nondiscriminatory multifactored assessment: A sourcebook.* New York: Human Sciences Press.

Barnett, D. & Zucker, K. (1985). Best practices in personality assessment. In J. Grimes & A. Thomas (Eds.), *Best practices manual* (pp. 1–16). Washington, DC: National Association of School Psychologists.

Block, J. H. & Block, J. (1980). The role of ego-control and ego-resiliency in the organization of behavior. In W. A. Collins (Ed.), *Development of cognition, affect, and social relations.* Hillsdale, NJ: Erlbaum.

Brim, O. G., & Kagan, J. (1980). *Constancy and change in human development.* Cambridge, MA: Harvard University Press.

Brubakken, D. M., Derouin, J. A., & Morrison, H. L. (1980). *Treatment of psychotic and neurologically impaired children: A systems approach.* New York: Van Nostrand Reinhold.

Burisch, M. (1984). Approaches to personality inventory construction. *American Psychologist, 39* (3), 214–227.

Cleveland, S. E. (1976). Reflections on the rise and fall of psychodiagnosis. *Professional Psychology, 7*, 309–318.

Dielman, T., & Barton, K. (1983). *Child personality structure and development: Multivariate theory and research.* New York: Praeger.

D'Zurilla, T. J., & Goldfried, M. R. (1971). Problem solving and behavior modification. *Journal of Abnormal Psychology, 78*, 107–126.

Edelbrock, C. (1983). Problems and issues in using rating scales to assess child personality and psychopathology. *School Psychology Review, 12*, 293–299.

Ellett, C. D., & Bersoff, D. N. (1976). An integrated approach to the psychosituational assessment of behavior. *Professional Psychology, 7*, 485–494.

Epstein, S. (1984). The stability of behavior across time and situations. In R. A. Zucker, J. Aronoff, & A. I. Rabin (Eds.), *Personality and the prediction of behavior* (pp. 209–268). Orlando, FL: Academic Press.

Garber, J. (1984). Classification of childhood psychopathology: A developmental perspective. *Child Development, 55*, 30–48.

Garfield, S. L., & Kurtz, R. (1977). A study of eclectic views. *Journal of Consulting and Clinical Psychology, 45*, 78–83.

Glenwick, D. S., & Jason, C. A. (1984). Locus of intervention in child cognitive behavior therapy: Implications of a behavioral community perspective. In A. W. Meyers & W. E. Craighead (Eds.), *Cognitive behavior therapy with children.* (pp. 129–162). New York: Plenum.

Goh, D. S., & Fuller, G. B. (1983). Current practices in the assessment of personality and behavior by school psychologists. *School Psychology Review, 12*, 240–243.

Goldfried, M. R. & Kent, R. N. (1972). Traditional versus behavioral personality assessment: A comparison of methodological and theoretical assumptions. *Psychological Bulletin, 77,* 409–420.

Gresham, F. M. (1984). Behavioral interviews in school psychology: Issues in psychometric adequacy and research. *School Psychology Review, 13,* 17–25.

Hall, C. S., & Lindzey, G. (1978). *Theories of personality* (3rd. ed.). New York: Wiley.

Hartman, A. (1978). Diagrammatic assessment of family relationships. *Social Casework,* October, 465–476.

Hawkins, R. P. (1979). The functions of assessment: Implications for selection and development of devices for assessing repertoires in clinical, educational, and other settings. *Journal of Applied Behavior Analysis, 12,* 501–516.

Hobbs, N. (1966). Helping disturbed children: Psychological and ecological strategies. *American Psychologist, 21,* 1105–1115.

Hobbs, N. (1979). *Helping disturbed children: Psychological and ecological strategies, II; Project Re-ed, twenty years later.* Nashville, TN: Center for the Study of Families and Children, Vanderbilt Institute for Public Policy Studies, Vanderbilt University.

Hogan, R., DeSoto, C. B., & Solano, C. (1977). Traits, tests and personality research. *American Psychologist, 32,* 255–264.

Ickes, W. (1984). Personality. In A. S. Bellack & M. Hersen (Eds.), *Research methods in clinical psychology* (pp. 157–178). New York: Pergamon.

Kanfer, F. H., & Saslow, G. (1969). Behavioral diagnosis. In C. Franks (Ed.), *Behavior therapy: appraisal and status* (pp. 417–444). New York: McGraw-Hill.

Kendall, P. C., & Hollon, S. D. (Eds.). (1981). *Assessment strategies for cognitive behavioral interventions.* New York: Academic Press.

Korchin, S. J., & Schuldberg, D. (1981). The future of clinical assessment. *American Psychologist, 36* (10), 1147–1158.

Ladd, G. W., & Mize, J. (1983). A cognitive-social learning model of social-skill training. *Psychological Review, 90,* 127–157.

Lanyon, R. I., & Goodstein, L. D. (1982). *Personality assessment* (2nd ed.). New York: Wiley.

Laosa, L. M., & Sigel, I. E. (Eds.). (1982). *Families as learning environments for children.* New York: Plenum.

McDermott, P. A. (1981). Sources of error in the psychoeducational diagnosis of children. *Journal of School Psychology, 19* (1), 31–44.

Mahoney, M. J. (1974). *Cognition and behavior modification.* Cambridge, MA: Ballinger.

Meichenbaum, D. (1977). *Cognitive-behavior modification.* New York: Plenum.

Meichenbaum, D., & Bowers, K. S. (1984). Introduction. In K. S. Bowers & D. Meichenbaum (Eds.), *The unconscious reconsidered* (pp. 1–8). New York: Wiley.

Meichenbaum, D. & Gilmore, J. B. (1984). The nature of unconscious processes: A cognitive-behavioral perspective. In K. S. Bowers & D. Meichenbaum (Eds.), *The unconscious reconsidered* (pp. 273–298). New York: Wiley.

Messick, S. (1983). Assessment of children. In P. H. Mussen (Ed.), *Handbook of child psychology* (Vol. 1, pp. 477–526). New York: Wiley.

Michelson, L., Sugai, D. P, Wood, R. P., & Kazdin, A. E. (1983). *Social skills assessment and training with children: An empirically based handbook.* New York: Plenum.

Mischel, W. (1968). *Personality and assessment.* New York: Wiley.

Mischel, W. (1973). Toward a cognitive social learning reconceptualization of personality. *Psychological Review, 80,* 252–283.

Mischel, W. (1981). A cognitive-social learning approach to assessment. In T. V. Merluzzi, C. R. Glass, & M. Genest (Eds.), *Cognitive assessment* (pp. 479–502). New York: Guilford.

Mischel, W. (1984). On the predictability of behavior and the structure of personality. In R. A. Zucker, J. Aronoff, & A. I. Rabin (Eds.), *Personality and the prediction of behavior* (pp. 269–305). New York: Academic Press.

Nisbett, R., & Ross, L. (1980). *Human inference: Strategies and shortcomings of social judgment.* Englewood Cliffs, NJ: Prentice-Hall.

Peterson, D. R. (1968). *The clinical study of social behavior.* New York: Appleton-Century-Crofts.

Phillips, L., Draguns, J. G., & Bartlett, D. P. (1975). Classification of behavior disorders. In N. Hobbs (Ed.), *Issues in the classification of children* (Vol. 1, pp. 26–55). San Francisco: Jossey-Bass.

Rapoport, J. L., & Ismond, D. R. (1984). *DSM-III training guide for diagnosis of childhood disorders.* New York: Brunner/Mazel.

Roberts, R. N., & Nelson, R. O. (1984). Assessment issues and strategies in cognitive behavior therapy with children. In A. W. Meyers & W. E. Craighead (Eds.), *Cognitive behavior therapy with children* (pp. 99–128). New York: Plenum.

Runyan, W. McK. (1983). Idiographic goals and methods in the study of lives. *Journal of Personality, 51,* 413–437.

Rutter, M. (1981). Stress, coping and development: Some issues and some questions. *Journal of Child Psychology and Psychiatry, 22,* 323–356.

Salvia, J., & Ysseldyke, J. E. (1981). *Assessment in remedial and special education* (2nd ed.). Boston: Houghton Mifflin.

Schön, D. A. (1983). *The reflective practitioner: How professionals think in action.* New York: Basic Books.

Sloves, R. E., Docherty, E. M., & Schneider, K. C. (1979). A scientific problem-solving model of psychological assessment. *Professional Psychology, 10,* 28–35.

Stagner, R. (1984). Trait psychology. In N. S. Endler & J. McV. Hunt (Eds.), *Personality and the behavior disorders* (2nd ed.) (Vol. 1, pp. 3–38). New York: Wiley.

Sugarman, A. (1978). Is psychodiagnostic assessment humanistic? *Journal of Personality Assessment, 42,* 11–21.

Wade, T. C., & Baker, T. B. (1977). Opinions and use of psychological tests. *American Psychologist, 32,* 874–882.

Werner, E. E. (1982). Sources of support for high-risk children. In N. J. Anastasiow, W. K. Frankenburg, & A. W. Fandal (Eds.), *Identifying the developmentally delayed child* (pp. 13–29). Baltimore, MD: University Park Press.

Wiener, I. B. (1972). Does psychodiagnosis have a future? *Journal of Personality Assessment, 36,* 534–546.

Weiner, I. B. (1983). The future of psychodiagnosis revisited. *Journal of Personality Assessment, 47,* 451–459.

Wiggins, J. S. (1973). *Personality and prediction: Principles of personality assessment.* Reading, MA: Addison-Wesley.

Wirt, R. D., Lachar, D., Klinedinst, J. K., & Seat, P. D. (1984). *Multidimensional description of personality: A manual for the personality inventory for children* (rev. ed.). Los Angeles: Western Psychological Services.

Preschool Assessment: Where Have We Been and Where Are We Going?

Carol Schneider Lidz

United Cerebral Palsy Association
of Philadelphia and Vicinity

ABSTRACT. This article reviews trends in the assessment of preschool children. Preschool assessment is compared with the assessment of other populations and early history, current status, recent advances, and future needs are discussed. Preschool assessment is seen as having both similarities with and important differences from other types of assessment. Though the last two decades have seen changes in models, procedures, and theories, it is concluded that much remains to be accomplished.

As the single representative of preschool assessment among the wide and varied array of assessment models and techniques discussed in this volume, it may be useful to begin with a Binet-like question: In what way is preschool assessment the same as other approaches, and in what way is it different? The answer to this question will provide a framework for addressing the more specific mission of this article, a discussion of the current status, recent advances, and suggested future developments in preschool assessment. As used in this article, the term *preschool* applies to children between the ages of two and five years.

SIMILARITIES

Any assessment is most fruitfully viewed as an aid to the decision-making process (see, e.g., Lidz, 1984). The decisions to

Requests for reprints should be sent to: Carol S. Lidz, Head Start Clinic Team, United Cerebral Palsy Association of Philadelphia, 4700 Wissahickon Ave., Philadelphia, PA 19144.

be made are generally similar across populations: Is the child eligible to enter or exit a program or treatment? Does the child deviate sufficiently from the norm to require intervention? What is the nature of the child's deviations and areas of adequacy? What are the appropriate interventions? How is the child progressing in a program or in response to a treatment, and what should the next step be? How is the child best approached within any particular setting?

The procedures and models used in preschool assessment are similar to and different from those used in the assessment of other populations. The differences often lie in emphasis rather than kind. Most practitioners appear to function in terms of an eclectic model where procedures vary in response to referral issues and setting. Such an eclectic model includes, when appropriate, concern with cause, description of the child's adequacies and deficiencies, a view of the child in context, and derivation of implications for intervention. Data sources for the model include observation, interview, questionnaire/rating scale, norm- and criterion-referenced standardized measures, and informal procedures. Though the specific content of the assessment varies in response to the age of the child, the nature of the approaches available is similar across populations.

The importance of the referral-initiated, individually-focused assessment does not seem to have diminished, although there has been increasing awareness of the role of contextual variables and an emphasis on an "ecological" approach to conducting the assessment and interpreting the results. Despite criticisms of focus on the individual, particularly in terms of diagnosing underlying etiology, both teachers and parents continue to request advice and intervention in relation to individuals, and it is unlikely that assessment of individuals will disappear as an area of concern for the professional diagnostician. What seems most likely to vary are the models, the instruments, the areas of focus, and the interpretation of data, with a broadening of the psychologist's role into program and system-related decision-making (Anderson, Cancelli, & Kratochwill, 1984).

DIFFERENCES

As indicated above, differences between preschool assessment and assessment of other populations are more often in emphasis than kind. Nonetheless, these differences are important (Lidz, 1983b). For example, although there has been a general concern with context and ecology in assessment, taking account of these variables and their effects on the preschool child is particularly important. For one, young children are at a time in their lives when they could be considered especially vulnerable to their environments. Second, because of language and cognitive limitations, preschool children cannot effectively report their experiences; therefore, greater reliance is placed on observation and reports from representatives in securing information about the child. Though data from representatives has its liabilities, in the case of observation at least, the unselfconscious spontaneity of most children minimizes potential observer effects. Finally, the inconsistency of some behaviors across tasks and situations often found with young children (Vane & Motta, 1980) emphasizes the importance of obtaining multiple samples in a variety of settings.

In addition to the importance of context, developmental stages play a unique role in preschool assessment. Young children are caught up in stage-related aspects of biological development which provide a unique basis for normative comparison.

Also relevant for assessment is the importance of play. Play can be used to assess cognitive, social, and affective development, as well as to reveal emotional content. Play comes naturally to young children; it is something most children can't help doing even when observed. When it does not occur, professionals should be concerned.

Finally, prediction of future status and diagnosis of etiology are of special importance at preschool ages. Young children usually have no school history and family history is often difficult to substantiate in any meaningful detail. Assessors of preschool children may be the first nonfamily member to interact with the child, and are therefore in good position to identify risk factors before significant difficulties to later adaptation develop.

SPECIFIC AREAS OF ASSESSMENT: WHERE HAVE WE BEEN AND WHERE ARE WE GOING?

Cognitive Assessment

One way to think about where we have been in the area of cognitive assessment is to review the progression of the most frequently used preschool cognitive tests: the Stanford-Binet Intelligence Scale (Terman & Merrill, 1972), the Wechsler Preschool and Primary Scale of Intelligence (Wechsler, 1967), the McCarthy Scales of Children's Abilities (McCarthy, 1972), and the Kaufman Assessment Battery for Children (K-ABC) (Kaufman & Kaufman, 1983). What does the widespread use of these tests tell us about our approach to the cognitive assessment of preschool children? First, it tells us that we determine cognitive deviance and normality by comparing a child with his or her peers. Second, with the exception of the K-ABC, it suggests little concern with what intelligence is, other than a simplistic notion that those who have more of "it" do better in school. Finally, with the possible exceptions of the Binet and the K-ABC, it suggests a failure to recognize that cognitive functioning of the young child changes qualitatively over relatively short periods of time. In general, these measures fail to reflect the research of Piaget and other developmental psychologists regarding cognitive functioning.

Before proceeding further, it should be made clear that there is no intent to dismiss the Binet or the McCarthy Scales, but only to raise questions about the use of these popular measures. The above list briefly summarizes what we are currently doing when we assess a child with the traditional repertoire of instruments. What, then, do we need to know about cognitive functioning and its assessment, and how much closer do newly-developed measures such as the K-ABC bring us to these answers?

First, we need to more satisfactorily define intelligence, especially as it pertains to assessment. There is continuing debate regarding the validity of global versus multiple intelligences (e.g., Gardner, 1983). Judging from the measures developed, there appears to be a consensus against the utility of a single, global IQ score, though the notion of a large, general intellectual component remains. But, what are the essential components of intellectual functioning as they relate to culturally and cross-culturally defined tasks, and is school achievement an adequate criterion with which to determine these components?

For preschool children, there is particular need to determine meaningful precursors of later development. For example, what does it *really* mean to note that a child can build a tower of six cubes? What this means now is that the child compares favorably with children of one age but not another. But, what does this behavior represent about the child's cognitive structures? What implications does this have for his or her future? What does a failure to display this behavior imply? Such information is essential to determining an educational program. What we do now is to go directly from the observation that the child cannot build a tower of six cubes to the recommendation that the child be taught how to do this.

How much closer do newly-developed measures, in particular the K-ABC, bring us to our quest? The K-ABC is the only attempt besides Piagetian measures to base a preschool cognitive test on an explicit theory of intelligence, albeit, omitting an important component of intelligence as defined by that theory (Das, 1984). The K-ABC attempts to promote a direct connection between assessment and intervention, the success of which remains to be determined. It has been successful in minimizing racial and socio-economic class differences, while maintaining a normative approach to the determination of cognitive functioning (Kaufman & Kaufman, 1983). For young, lower functioning preschoolers, the floor of the test is insufficient, but it is an easily administered, attractive test for the mildly impaired or higher functioning preschooler (see special issue of the *Journal of Special Education*, 1984, *18* (3) for further critique and discussion). Though, the K-ABC appears to minimize the effects of experience, it does not directly address the issue of the extent to which the child's cognitive structures are modifiable. Thus, the K-ABC is traditional in its approach. It falls short of providing responses to questions of learning "potential" and hypotheses for remediation beyond those that can be categorized into the test's simultaneous versus sequential processing dimensions. As a representative of a traditional norm-based approach to assessment, though, the K-ABC makes a positive contribution in its sophisticated psychometrics, functions tapped, relevance for young children, and attempts to define what it measures.

Assessment of Adaptive Behavior

The assessment of adaptive behavior raises additional issues and questions for preschool assessment. Where we have been is fairly easily summarized by the mention of two measures: the Vineland Social Maturity Scale (Doll, 1965) and the Adaptive Behavior Scale (Lambert, Windmiller, Tharinger, & Cole, 1981). It is interesting that most definitions of intelligence include some mention or implication regarding adaptation, but, in assessment, adaptive behavior is somehow viewed as an entity distinguishable from intelligence. A child cannot be classified as retarded without both kinds of measures, but these measures are discussed in separate terms. Presumably, adaptive behavior estimates functioning in the environment, a kind of "activities of daily living" assessment (Coulter & Morrow, 1978). There has been a recent onslaught of new adaptive behavior measures (e.g., Bruinicks, 1984; Leland, Shodee, McElwain & Christie, 1980; Sparrow, Balla & Cicchetti, 1984), but when specific items and domains are analyzed with respect to the young child, what is being measured is either fine motor ability, self help skill, or overlap with what IQ tests assess.

Is this what we need? Information about self help is arguably an area of interest and relevance in planning for the young child, but missing from these measures and only included in the psychometrically questionable Children's Adaptive Behavior Scale (Richmond & Kicklighter, 1980), is an indicator of out-of-school problem solving abilities. This type of measure would yield an assessment of cognitive functioning which would more closely relate intelligence to real life demands rather than school achievement and would hold promise for separating the low-achieving streetwise child from the child with generally deficient cognitive functioning. In order to do this, a directly-administered procedure which assesses problem solving strategies and coping abilities in everyday tasks would be most desirable (see Zeitlin's 1978 Coping Inventory for another attempt in this direction).

An example of an assessment procedure which bridges cognitive assessment with adaptive-like behavior has been developed by Feuerstein (1979) and his co-workers in Israel. This is called dynamic assessment (see paper in this volume). Though dynamic assessment has not yet been applied to young children, the model is appropriate, and development of procedures for preschool children is currently underway (Lidz, 1983a; Tsuriel & Klein, in press). Dynamic procedures place the examiner in the role of intervener within a test-teach-test model which assumes that cognitive functions are identifiable and modifiable. The outcome of a dynamic assessment is an estimate of the modifiability of the learner, elaboration of cognitive strengths and deficiencies, and hypotheses about effective remedial strategies. Dynamic assessment, as a viable addition to the assessment repertoire, is still in its infancy, but offers the promise of a genuinely unique supplement to current static measures that are better able to respond to questions of *what* than of *how* or *why*.

Piagetian Measures

Despite the impact of Piaget's work on child development theory as well as on curriculum practice, his work has had minimal influence on the assessment of preschool children. Among those measures that attempt to incorporate Piaget's work, the Uzgiris and Hunt Scales (1975) are limited to infants, the Wachs Analysis of Cognitive Structures (Wachs & Vaughan, 1977), although relevant to most preschool curricula, is discernably Piagetian only in its written introduction, and the Laurendeau and Pinard (1977) measures are for French Canadians. Derivations of Piaget's work are evident in specific test items of the arithmetic scale of the K-ABC, and there have been some Piaget-based research measures, such as the one developed by Goldschmid and Bentler (1968). However, little else has appeared for the assessment of preschool children.

Would the development of Piagetian measures be a worthwhile direction for the future? This author would offer a qualified "yes". The hesitation relates to the limited information provided by such measures. The stages defined by Piaget's work are fairly gross, and Piaget, who was primarily interested in the *study* of development, never intended his measures to be used for inter-individual discrimination or intra-individual assessment (Dunst & Gallagher, 1983). Such measures also do not have a clear link with intervention, but rather offer another type of normative estimate. However, existing evidence suggests that Piagetian measures are less sensitive to race, socioeconomic factors, and bilingualism than current tests (Clarizio, 1982). Piagetian measures also have the advantage of being tied to a theory of intellectual development and, therefore, may reflect something more "real" about the child's functioning than current tests. Finally, they show promise in reflecting gains in response to intervention and would be helpful in program evaluation.

Assessment of Achievement

Where we have been in the assessment of preschool achievement relates closely to Project Head Start and to other model early intervention programs. There is much in the area of achievement assessment which is best described as informal, and, as in the discussion of cognitive assessment, the past and present can largely be summarized by the mention of specific tests. Two significant measures are the Caldwell Preschool Inventory, or Cooperative Preschool Inventory (Caldwell, 1970), and the Boehm Test of Basic Concepts (Boehm, 1969). Criterion-referenced measures, such as the Learning Accomplishment Profile (Sanford, 1974), have also been widely used as have similar tests developed by various preschool projects around the country. The extent to which these measures are truly criterion-referenced, however, is open to question (see Lidz, 1981). Two recent tests show particular promise for assessing achievement and far surpass the technical quality of past methods: these are the Developmental Tasks for Kindergarten Readiness (Lesiak, 1978) and the Bracken Scale of Basic Concepts (Bracken, 1984).

Thus, where we have gone in the area of assessment of preschool achievement is towards technical improvement: that is, toward development of measures which are more psychometrically sound. These new tests are generally referenced to most preschool or kindergarten curriculum content. What we do not yet have are measures which reflect not only the end states of knowledge, but the strategies and styles relevant to knowledge acquisition and application. One attempt to assess at least one aspect of this (viz. attention to task by means of direct observation) is offered by the Preacademic Behavior Code (Durgan, 1980).

Assessment of Social and Emotional Functioning

Social and emotional functioning are both strongly related to cognitive growth and appear to follow a similar sequence of development (e.g., Shantz, 1975). The assessment of the social and emotional functioning of preschool children differs from assessment in areas already discussed in that there is greater recognition of the importance of theory. In total, however, very few measures have been produced in this important area (Fewell, 1983; Gresham & Elliott, 1984; Guralnick & Weinhouse, 1983).[1] Variations of both psychodynamic and social/learning theory interpretations of behavior have been incorporated in interviews, classroom observations, play sessions, or projective techniques. What we have now are some procedures which derive from research, such as Lewis and

---

[1]See Walker (1973) for a review of measures.

Michalson's (1983) observational scale of emotional functioning for children birth to three, a Canadian social competency observational measure which reflects the research of Burton White (Wright, 1983), the temperament measures based upon the investigations of Thomas, Chess, and Birch (Keogh, Pullis, & Caldwell, 1982; Thomas & Chess, 1977; Thomas, Chess, & Birch, 1968), social problem solving measures (Krasnor & Rubin, 1981; Shure & Spivack, 1978), and the beginnings of some empirically-derived standardized questionnaire procedures. A particularly interesting example of a questionnaire procedure is the Test of Early Socioemotional Development (Hresko & Brown, 1984), which assesses social and emotional functioning as determined by four sources of information: a teacher rating scale, a parent rating scale, a student rating scale, and a sociometric peer nominating technique. This is a standardized, normed measure which the authors describe as ecological, since it simultaneously looks at the home, school, and the individual. The TOESD (minus the sociometric technique) is impressive in the representativeness of its standardization sample, its high test-retest reliabilities, and in the results of early validity studies.

Direct observation, or behavioral assessment, remains a viable approach to evaluation of problematic social interaction or emotional expression. However, most observational approaches, though appropriate to preschool settings, are general and not referral-specific (e.g., Carden-Smith, 1980; Gottfried & Seay, 1973; Wahler, House, & Stambaugh, 1976); some, such as time and event sampling approaches, can become very time consuming relative to the amount of information yielded. Many professionals still rely upon informal observation guided by behaviors of concern as specified by the teacher, but, for those preferring a more formalized approach which is both referral-specific as well as practical, psycho-situational assessment is available. This is an event-sampling strategy which utilizes a behaviorally-based format of specifying target and terminal behaviors, and records frequency, duration, intensity, latency, and antecedent and consequent situations (for details, see Bersoff & Grieger, 1971; Ellet & Bersoff, 1976; Grieger & Abidin, 1972; and Lidz, 1981). The interested reader should consult Halle and Sindelar (1982) for a further discussion of behavioral observation methodologies applied to the classroom.

There is no single or simple assessment technique which will provide adequate answers to such complex issues as are presented by social and emotional functioning. The conscientious assessor can only apply a myriad of approaches, some formal, some informal, using questionnaires, tests, and observations that provide data for generating and testing hypotheses (Lidz, 1981).

What is needed in the area of social/emotional assessment are procedures which reflect research on developmental stages, allow the assessor to focus on specific behaviors of relevance to referral issues, and which yield implications for intervention. It is likely that direct observation will maintain its status as the most relevant source of information for the foreseeable future.

Both assessment of parent/child interaction and utilization of play procedures are relevant to the discussion of social and emotional functioning, but, because each of these represents a relatively unique and developing area of assessment for young children, separate discussion is offered.

Assessment of Parent/Child Interaction

Unlike the areas of assessment discussed thus far, the assessment of parent/child interaction represents an attempt to relate means and processes to the end products of functioning. The assessor's interest is most frequently in the relationship between parent/child interaction and either cognitive or social/emotional behaviors, and the concern is both to formulate hypotheses of possible cause, as well as to propose directions for intervention. Also relatively unique to this area is the extensive amount of research with relatively few attempts to apply research methods to assessment practice. Increased interest in assessment of these interactions reflects an awareness of the need to conduct assessments and deliver interventions which acknowledge the central role of the parent in the functioning of the young, developing child (Dunst, 1983). Feuerstein's hypotheses about the importance of mediated learning experiences for cognitive development have helped to increase awareness of the relevance of parent/child interaction in assessment, and researchers such as Klein, in association with Feuerstein (in press) are developing standardized observation procedures which specifically focus on the quality and nature of such experiences. Research on the relationship of parenting style to emotional dependence and socialization skill (e.g. Garwood & Page, 1979) has also influenced assessment measures.

Other observational procedures under development include those by Budd, Riner, and Brockman (in press) regarding parent management of problem behaviors; Cole and St. Clair-Stokes (1984), who focus on facilitation of communication; Erickson's procedure (Erickson, Sroufe, & Egelund, in press) which assesses the ability of the child to use the parent as a resource and the parent's ability to foster independence and competence; Farran's (Farran, Kasari, Yoder, Harber, Huntington, & Comfort-Smith, 1984), which offers an approach to rating general quality of parent/child interaction; Guinagh and Jester (1982), who present an informal checklist to evaluate how parents read to their children; Russo and Owens (1982) who assess parental strategies related to interactional communication and language stimulation; and Toub's (1978) fifteen-minute diagnostic screening for emotional disturbance. Finally, a procedure which is commercially available and is in self-report questionnaire format, is the Parent as Teacher Inventory by Strom (1984). Some preliminary research on this measure is reviewed and reported by Strom and Slaughter (1978).

All of the procedures listed in this section are in a formative stage and require considerable research to demonstrate their utility. However, there is sufficient indication of awareness of the need for such measures. The focus so far has included parental behaviors which stimulate cognitive and communication competence, those which are primarily concerned with behavior management and emotional responsiveness, and those which look at the parent in the role of teacher. In many cases, the nature and role of the child in these interactions is acknowledged and assessed. What is not always clear are the processes which need to be looked at during the course of parent/child interactons. Klein and Feuerstein (in press) are among the few who offer not just an empirical, but a theoretical basis for their observations. A related area where there is a clear gap is the assessment of teacher/child interactions at the preschool level. Measures of teacher behaviors would be extremely useful both in terms of group management techniques relating to cognitive and social/emotional functioning, as well as teacher interactions in communication dyads with individual children.

Assessment of Play

Play has long been valued by analytically-oriented therapists as the window to the emotions of the child (e.g., Alexander, 1958; Peller, 1955). There is a long tradition in the treatment of children using play for both diagnosis and intervention, with interpretations based on the hypothetical formulations derived from psychodynamic theory. With time and the investigations of Piaget, there has been increased interest in play as a window to cognitive and social development as well (e.g., Fewell, 1983).

An early attempt at assessment of children's play was the Driscoll Play Kit (Driscoll, no date), which provided virtually no standardization or normative information, but merely presented a durable set of miniature toys for the use of diagnosticians, therapists, and researchers. There are a number of contemporary attempts to develop standardized assessment approaches, including the Cooperative Play Code (Cooper, 1980), assessment of free play behavior (Clune, Paolella, & Foley, 1979), the Play Assessment Scale (Fewell, 1984), the Goodman Lock Box (Goodman, 1981), the analysis of play behavior to diagnose neurological impairment (Gordon, White & Diller, 1972), and the Symbolic Play Test (Lowe & Costello, 1976). The most impressive of these is the Goodman Lock Box, which is commercially available. In this approach, children are presented with a large wood box with ten doors in two rows of five. Each door is secured with a lock of varying degrees of difficulty, behind which is a toy. The examiner scores every move of the child which occurs within six and a half minutes of the initial presentation of the box, and derives scores indicative of the level of the child's cognitive functioning. The scoring is relatively easy, and a training tape is available for purchase. The test was normed on Philadelphia children with a wide variety of socioeconomic backgrounds and shows promise as a nondiscriminatory means of differentiating retarded from nonretarded levels of functioning.

Measures of play typically assess the child in interaction with objects, in contrast to social/affective measures which assess children in interaction with people. Whereas focus on the child's isolated interaction with objects is appropriate for the very young child, the preschooler nearing age four and five is a very social creature. An improvement of both play and social measures would extend to focus beyond object relatedness and include observations of behavior in a social context. Play in a group would also be the only means of viewing the continuum of isolated to parallel to cooperative play interaction, as well as allowing expression of dramatic, imaginative behaviors as a reflection of symbolic capacity.

Assessing the Environment

There has been an increase in advocacy of an ecological approach to assessment in general as well as in approaches to research on developmental processes (Bronfenbrenner, 1976; Carlson, Scott, & Eklund, 1980; Wicker, 1979). Such an approach is relevant to assessment of the preschool child. Mulliken and Buckley (1983) comment that "ecological assessment sees and assesses the individual in a variety of settings using a multidisciplinary approach . . . It recognizes that each child . . . operates on and influences his environment as well as being influenced by it" (p. 49). According to such a point of view, the assessors would observe the child interacting in a variety of contexts, and would consider the demands made by the task, the child's early history, social and educational environments, and the characteristics of the child.

One environment in which potentially valuable information could be gathered is the home. Though it would be ideal to spend a substantial amount of time in the child's home observing the many interactions as well as the physical variables of that environment, few assessors are able to take the time, or perhaps even feel comfortable, doing this. For those who are able to make a home visit, one relevant assessment tool is the Home Observation for Measurement of the Environment (HOME) by Caldwell and Bradley (1978). Freund, Bradley, and Caldwell (1979) offer a review of earlier measures of home environment as well as of research specifically involving the HOME. For those not able to assess the home environment directly, the Home Screening Questionnaire (Coons, Gay, Fandal, Ker, & Frankenburg, 1981), standardized on a low-SES population, uses items selected from the HOME inventory, and presents these in questionnaire format for the parent to complete. Preliminary research described by the authors is generally favorable in terms of agreement with the original HOME, although the agreement level for low HOME scores is not as favorable as for high scores.

CONCLUSION

There continue to be several unresolved issues associated with the assessment of preschool children. One such issue is the ongoing dissatisfaction with labeling and with inadequately established relationships between diagnosis and treatment (Hobbs, 1975). For example, the definition of learning disability used in PL 94-142 allows school systems to deny children in an "at risk" status any intervention until they have experienced a sufficiently observable amount of failure. Within the Head Start system, children who manifest developmental delays which cannot be clearly defined or assessed must be classified as mentally retarded, specific learning disability, or speech impaired in order to receive needed services, and children with social and emotional problems can gain this help only with a label of serious emotional disturbance. New and more meaningful approaches to classification need to be established. Greenspan (Greenspan, 1981; Greenspan & Lourie, 1981) has made a beginning in rethinking this issue for the infant. Hobbs (1975) recommended that classification be linked to "services required, not types of children; it should link etiology, current status, intervention, and outcome . . . it should include the matrix of other persons significant in the life of the child, as well as settings; and it should be dated and its validity bound to a limited period of time" (p. 234). We remain far from these goals.

There is also the issue of whether those currently assessing preschool children are fully qualified. Many professionals appear to be conducting preschool assessment who are not completely comfortable with young children. There is, however, an increased awareness of the need to be specifically educated about and experienced with this population (Ulrey & Schnell, 1982). Assessment and intervention with preschoolers are complex tasks that warrant specialized courses and degree programs. (see Boehm & Sandberg, 1982; Goodwin & Goodwin, 1982; Keogh, 1982; McCall, 1981; Palmer, 1983).

In view of the special issues and problems of assessing the young child, a multidisciplinary, multi-variate approach is essential (Simeonsson, Huntington & Parse, 1980). Because prediction of future status and determination of program effectiveness remain precarious ventures, the special-needs child requires ongoing monitoring and frequent reassessment. A one-session, one-assessor, one-test approach is insufficient to grasp the nature of the child's functioning or to determine directions for remediation. Both norm- and criterion-referenced measures have been found to be insufficient *in and of themselves* (Lidz, 1981, 1979). No single approach can respond to all the relevant assessment questions.

There has been increased recognition in the last two decades of the complexity involved in assessing children of any age and of the preschooler in particular (Messick, 1983). This recognition has led to the search for alternative approaches such as dynamic procedures, theory-based tests with implications for intervention, ecological models, and ongoing monitoring of progress (Ysseldyke, 1982). Perhaps what has been most promising over the last several years are the signs of change and the proposals for alternatives. Such changes are no longer limited to the appearance of a new test within an old model; the models themselves and our basic assumptions are being questioned. Out of this inquiry there is the hope for positive development.

REFERENCES

Alexander, F. (1958). A contribution to the theory of play. *Psychoanalytic Quarterly, 27,* 175–193.

Anderson, T. K., Cancelli, A. A., and Kratochwill, T. R. (1984). Self-reported assessment practices of school psychologists: Implications for training and practice. *Journal of School Psychology, 22,* 17–29.

Bersoff, D. N. and Grieger, R. M. (1971). An interview model for the psychosituational assessment of children's behavior. *American Journal of Orthopsychiatry, 41,* 483–493.

Boehm, A. E. (1969). *Boehm Test of Basic Concepts.* New York: The Psychological Corporation.

Boehm, A. E. and Sandberg, B. R. (1982). Assessment of the preschool child. In C. R. Reynolds and T. B. Gutkin (Eds.). *The handbook of school psychology* (pp. 82–120). New York: John Wiley and Sons.

Bracken, B. A. (1984). *Bracken Basic Concept Scale.* Columbus, OH: Charles E. Merrill.

Bronfenbrenner, U. (1976). *Reality and research in the ecology of human development.* Washington, D. C.: American Psychological Association, Master Lectures on Developmental Psychology, Ms. 1333.

Bruininks, R. H., Woodcock, R. W., Weatherman, R. F., and Hill, B. K. (1984). *Scales of Independent Behavior: Woodcock-Johnson Psycho-Educational Battery, Part 4.* Allen, Texas: DLM Teaching Resources.

Budd, K. S., Riner, L. S. and Brockman, M. P. (in press). A structured observation system for clinical evaluation of parent training.

Caldwell, B. M. (1970). *Cooperative Preschool Inventory.* Reading, MA: Addison-Wesley Publishing Co.

Caldwell, B. M. and Bradley, R. H. (1978). *Home Observation Measurement of the Environment Manual.* Little Rock, AR: University of Arkansas.

Carden-Smith, L. (1980). *Classroom observation code: Covariation between child behavior problems and classroom format variables.* Lawrence, KS: Kansas Early Childhood Institute.

Carlson, C. I., Scott, M., and Eklund, S. J. (1980). Ecological theory and method for behavioral assessment. *School Psychology Review, 9,* 75–82.

Clarizio, H. D. (1982). Piagetian measures revisited: Issues and applications. *Psychology in the Schools, 19,* 421–430.

Clune, C., Paolella, J. M. and Foley, J. M. (1979). Free-play behavior of atypical children: An approach to assessment. *Journal of Autism and Developmental Disorders, 9*(1), 61–71.

Cole, E. B. and St. Clair-Stokes, J. (1984). Caregiver-child interactive behaviors. A videotape analysis procedure *Volta Review*, *86*, 200–217.

Coons, C. E., Gay, E. C., Fandal, A. W., Ker, C., and Frankenburg, W. K. (1981). *The home screening questionnaire reference manual*. Denver, CO: John F. Kennedy Child Development Center, School of Medicine, University of Colorado Health Sciences Center.

Cooper, A. Y. (1980). *Cooperative play code: Cooperative play in an integrated preschool*. Lawrence, KS: Kansas Early Childhood Institute.

Coulter, W. A. and Morrow, H. W. (1978). *Adaptive behavior: Concepts and measurements*. New York: Grune and Stratton.

Das, J. P. (1984). Test review: Kaufman Assessment Battery for Children (K-ABC). *Journal of Psychoeducational Assessment*, *2*(1), 83–90.

Doll, E. (1965). *Vineland Social Maturity Scale*. Circle Pines, MN: American Guidance Service.

Driscoll, G. P. (no date). *The Driscoll Play Kit manual*. New York: The Psychological Corporation.

Dunst, C. J. (1983). Emerging trends and advances in early intervention programs. *New Jersey Journal of School Psychology*, *2*, 26–40.

Dunst, C. J. and Gallagher, J. L. (1983). Piagetian approaches to infant assessment. *Topics in Early Childhood Special Education*, *3*(1), 44–62.

Durgan, B. (1980). *Preacademic behavior code*. Lawrence, KS: Kansas Early Childhood Institute.

Ellett, C. D. and Bersoff, D. N. (1976). An integrated approach to the psychosituational assessment of behavior. *Professional Psychology*, *7*, 435–444.

Erickson, M. F., Sroufe, L. A., and Egelund, B. (in press). The relationship between quality of attachment and behavior problems in preschool in a high-risk sample. In I. Bretherton and E. Waters (Eds.). *Child Development Monographs*.

Farran, D. C., Kasari, C., Yoder, P., Harber, L., Huntington, G., and Comfort-Smith, M. (1984). *Rating mother-child interactions in handicapped and at-risk infants*. Paper presented at the First International Symposium on Intervention and Stimulation in Infant Development, Jerusalem.

Feuerstein, R. (1979). *The dynamic assessment of retarded performers*. Baltimore: University Park Press.

Feuerstein, R. (1980). *Instrumental enrichment*. Baltimore: University Park Press.

Fewell, R. R. (1983). New directions in the assessment of young handicapped children. In C. R. Reynolds and J. H. Clark (Eds.). *Assessment and programming for young children with low-incidence handicaps* (pp. 1–42). New York: Plenum Press.

Fewell, R. R. (1984). *Play Assessment Scale-fourth revision*. Seattle: University of Washington.

Freund, J. H., Bradley, R. H., and Caldwell, B. M. (1979). The home environment in the assessment of learning disabilities. *Learning Disability Quarterly*, *2*, 39–50.

Gardner, H. (1983). *Frames of mind: The theory of multiple intelligences*. New York: Basic Books.

Garwood, S. G. and Page, D. (1979). Acquiring social skills in early childhood. In S. G. Garwood (Ed.). *Educating young handicapped children: A developmental approach*. Germantown, MD: Aspen Systems Corporation.

Goldschmid, M. L. and Bentler, P. M. (1968). *Concept Assessment Kit: Conservation*. San Diego: Educational and Industrial Testing Service.

Goodman, J. F. (1981). *The Goodman Lock Box, instruction manual*. Chicago: Stoelting Co.

Goodwin, W. L. and Goodwin, L. D. (1982). Measuring young children. In B. Spodek (Ed.) (pp. 523–563). *Handbook of research in early childhood education*. New York: The Free Press.

Gordon, R., White, D., and Diller, L. (1972). Performance of neurologically impaired preschool children with educational materials. *Exceptional Children*, *39*, 428–437.

Gottfried, N. W. and Seay, B. (1973). An observational technique for preschool children. *Journal of Genetic Psychology, 122,* 263–268.

Greenspan, S. I. (1981). Adaptive and psychopathologic patterns in infancy and early childhood: An overview. *Children Today, 10*(4), 21–26.

Greenspan, S. and Lourie, R. S. (1981). Developmental structuralist approach to the classification of adaptive and pathological personality organizations: Infancy and early childhood. *American Journal of Psychiatry, 138,* 725–735.

Gresham, F. M. and Elliott, S.N. (1984). Assessment and classification of children's social skills: A review of methods and issues. *School Psychology Review, 13,* 292–301.

Grieger, R. M. and Abidin, R. R. (1972). Psychosocial assessment: A model for the school community psychologist. *Psychology in the Schools, 9,* 112–119.

Guralnick, M. J. and Weinhouse, E. (1983). Child-child social interactions: An analysis of assessment instruments for young children. *Exceptional Children, 50,* 268–271.

Guinagh, B. J. and Jester, R. E. (1972). How parents read to children. *Theory into Practice, 11,* 171–177.

Halle, J. W. and Sindelar, P. T. (1982). Behavioral observational methodologies for early childhood education. *Topics in Early Childhood Special Education, 2*(1), 43–54.

Hobbs, N. (1975). *The futures of children.* San Francisco: Jossey-Bass.

Hresko, W. P. and Brown, L. (1984). *Test of Early Socioemotional Development.* Austin: Pro-Ed.

Kaufman, A. S. and Kaufman, N. L. (1983). *Kaufman Assessment Battery for Children.* Circle Pine, MN: American Guidance Service.

Keogh, B. K. (Ed.). Early identification of children with potential learning problems. *Journal of Special Education, 4*(3), 307–363.

Keogh, B. K., Pullis, M. E. and Cadwell, J. (1982). A short form of the Teacher Temperament Questionnaire. *Journal of Educational Measurement, 19,* 323–329.

Klein, P. S. and Feuerstein, R. (in press). Environmental variables and cognitive development: Identification of the potent factors in adult-child interaction. In S. Harel, and N. J. Anostasiow (Eds.). *At risk infant: Psycho/socio/medical aspects.* New York: P. H. Brooks.

Krasnor, L. R. and Rubin, K. H. (1981). The assessmen of social problem-solving skills in young children. In T. V. Merlizzi, C. R. Glass, and M. Genest (Eds.) (pp. 452–476). *Cognitive assessment.* New York: The Guilford Press.

Lambert, N., Windmiller, M., Tharinger, D. and Cole, L. (1981). *AAMD Adaptive Behavior Scale, School edition.* Monterey, CA: Publishers Test Service (CTB/McGraw-Hill).

Laurendeau, M. and Pinard, A. (1977). *The development of the concept of space in the child.* New York: International Universities Press.

Leland, H., Shodee, M., McElwain, D., and Christie, R. (1980). *Adaptive Behavior Scale for Infants and Early Childhood.* Columbus, OH: Ohio State University, Nisonger Center.

Lewis, M. and Michalson, L. (1983). *Children's emotions and moods: Developmental theory and measurement.* New York: Plenum.

Lesiak, W. J., Jr. (1978). *Developmental Tasks for Kindergarten Readiness.* Brandon, VT: Clinical Psychology Publishing Co.

Lidz, C. S. (1979). Criterion-referenced assessment: The new bandwagon? *Exceptional Children, 46*(2), 131–132.

Lidz, C. S. (1981). *Improving assessment of school children. San Francisco: Jossey-Bass.*

Lidz, C. S. (1983a). Dynamic assessment and the preschool child. *Journal of Psychoeducational Assessment, 1*(1), 59–72.

Lidz, C. S. (1983b). Issues in assessing preschool children. In K. Paget and B. A. Bracken (Eds.). *Preschool assessment.* New York: Grune and Stratton.

Lidz, C. S. (1984). Educational assessment. In R. J. Corsini (Ed.). *Encyclopedia of psychology, volume I* (pp. 411–412). New York: John Wiley and Sons.

Lowe, M. and Costello, A. J. (1976). *Manual for the Symbolic Play Test, experimental edition.* Windsor, England: NFER-Nelson Publishing Co.

McCall, R. B. (1981). Issues in the early development of intelligence and its assessment. In M. Lewis and L. T. Taft (Eds.). *Developmental disabilities in preschool children: Theory assessment, and intervention.* New York: Spectrum Publications, Inc.

McCarthy, D. (1972). *McCarthy Scales of Children's Abilities.* New York: The Psychological Corporation.

Messick, S. (1983). Assessment of children. In P. Mussen (Ed.). *Handbook of child psychology: History, theory and methods* (4th ed., vol. 1). New York: John Wiley and Sons.

Mulliken, R. K. and Buckley, J. J. (1983). *Assessment of multihandicapped and developmentally disabled children.* Rockville, MD: Aspen Systems Corp.

Paget, K. and Bracken, B. A. (1983). *The psychoeducational assessment of preschool children.* New York: Grune and Stratton.

Palmer, J. O. (1983). *The psychological assessment of children* (pp. 445–460). New York: John Wiley and Sons.

Peller, L. E. (1955). Libidinal development as reflected in play. *Psychoanalysis, 3*(3), 3–12.

Richmond, B. W. and Kicklighter, R. H. (1980). *Children's Adaptive Behavior Scale.* Atlanta: Humanics.

Russo, J. B. and Owens, R. E., Jr. (1982). The development of an observation tool for parent-child interaction. *Journal of Speech and Hearing Disorders, 47,* 165–173.

Sanford, A. R. (1974). *Learning Accomplishment Profile.* Winston-Salem, N.C.: Kaplan Press.

Shantz, C. W. (1975). *The development of social cognition.* Chicago: University of Chicago Press.

Shure, M. and Spivak, G. (1978). *Problem solving techniques in child rearing.* San Francisco: Jossey-Bass.

Simeonsson, R. J., Huntington, G. S. and Parse, S. A. (1980). Expanding the developmental assessment of young handicapped children. In J. J. Gallagher (Ed.). *New directions for exceptional children, no. 3.* San Francisco: Jossey-Bass.

Sparrow, S. S., Balla, D. A. and Cicchetti, D. V. (1984). *Vineland Adaptive Behavior Scales.* Circle Pines, MN: American Guidance Service.

Strom, R. (1984). *Parent as a Teacher Inventory.* Bensenville, IL: Scholastic Testing Service.

Strom, R. and Slaughter, H. (1978). Measurement of childrearing expectations using the Parent as a Teacher Inventory. *Journal of Experimental Education, 46*(4), 44–53.

Terman, L. M. and Merrill, M. A. (1972). *Stanford-Binet Intelligence Scale.* Boston: Houghton Mifflin.

Thomas, A. and Chess, S. (1977). *Temperament and development.* New York: Brunner/Mazel.

Thomas, A., Chess, S., and Birch, H. (1968). *Temperament and behavior disorders in children.* New York: New York University.

Toub, G. S. (1978). A rapid assessment procedure for mother-child interactions. *Journal of Clinical Child Psychology, 7,* 132–135.

Tsuriel, D. and Klein, P. (in press). The assessment of analogical thinking modifiability among regular, special education disadvantaged and mentally retarded children. *Journal of Abnormal Child Psychology.*

Ulrey, G. and Schnell, R. R. (1982). Introduction to assessing young children. In G. Ulrey and S. J. Rogers (eds.). *Psychological assessment of handicapped infants and young children.* New York: Thieme-Stratton, Inc.

Uzgiris, I. and Hunt, J. McV. (1975). *Assessment in infancy: Ordinal scales of psychological development.* Urbana, IL: University of Illinois Press.

Vane, J. R. and Motta, R. W. (1980). Test response inconsistency in young children. *Journal of School Psychology, 18*(1), 25–33.

Wachs, H. and Vaughan, L. J. (1977). *Wachs Analysis of Cognitive Structures.* Los Angeles: Western Psychological Services.

Wahler, R. G., House, A. E. and Stambaugh, E. E., II. (1976). *Ecological Assessment of Child Problem Behavior.* New York: Pergamon Press.

Walker, D. K. (1973). *Socioemotional measures for preschool and kindergarten children.* San Francisco: Jossey-Bass.

Wechsler, D. (1967). *Manual for the Wechsler Preschool and Primary Scale of Intelligence.* New York: Psychological Corporation.

Wicker, Q. W. (1979). Ecological psychology: Some recent and prospective developments. *American Psychologist, 34,* 755–765.

Wright, M. J. (1983). *A Canadian approach: Compensatory education in the preschool. The University of Western Ontario Preschool Project.* Ypsilanti, MI: The High Scope Press.

Ysseldyke, J. E. (1982, August). *Planning instructional interventions: What does the research say?* Paper presented at the Annual Meeting of the American Psychological Association, Washington, D. C.

Zeitlin, S. (1978). *Coping Inventory-A measure of adaptive behavior.* Cliffside, N.J.: Innovative Educational Materials.

Toward Objective Diagnosis of Learning Disabilities

Cecil R. Reynolds

Texas A&M University

ABSTRACT. Considerable confusion and subjectivity has plagued the diagnosis of learning disabilities since the field was first established. Though clinical judgement is necessary for appropriate diagnosis and provision of services to learning disabled children, such judgement must be steeped in evidence and given clear empirical guidance. Application of the severe discrepancy criterion dictated in Federal regulations offers an excellent beginning point in objectifying learning disability diagnosis.

"Well, I think a learning disabled child is, well, they're, they're hard to describe exactly, *but I know one when I see one!*"

For many years the diagnosis and evaluation of learning disabilities has been a significant problem. Central to the issues involved has been the problem of arriving at a workable definition of learning disability (LD). Education and psychology, the primary fields concerned with learning disabilities are low consensus fields, dealing with human behavior and theoretical constructs (of which LD is one), and much controversy exists regarding just what constitutes a learning disability. There seem, at times, to be as many theories of etiology of LD as there are "stars in the sky." Equally as many variables seem to demand careful, compassionate consideration in defining LD.

Requests for reprints may be sent to Cecil R. Reynolds, Dept. of Educational Psychology, Texas A&M University, College Station, TX 77843.

This paper is based in part on the report of the United States Department of Education, Special Education Programs Work Group on Measurement Issues in the Assessment of Learning Disabilities. The members of this work group were Cecil R. Reynolds (chair), Ronald A. Berk, Gwyneth M. Boodoo, Jan Cox, Terry B. Gutkin, Lester Mann, Ellis B. Page, Victor L. Willson, and Frank L. Schmidt (advisor to the workgroup). The opinions expressed herein are those of the author and not policy or opinions of the USDE, Special Education Programs.

Two broad factors determine "who" is LD, (a) the definition of LD, and (b) how the definition is operationalized in practice. Debates over definitions of LD appear endless and Senf (1981) has provided an insightful discussion of why this is likely to continue. However much we need continued debate and discussion, lest the field grow stagnant, a statutory definition has been in place for nearly a decade, and it is the definition that must, by law, be implemented. The rules and regulations for implementation of PL 94-142 provide the following definition for use by multidisciplinary teams in deciding upon a diagnosis of LD. This definition states that a determination of LD is made based on (1) whether a child does not achieve commensurate with his or her age and ability when provided with appropriate educational experiences, and (2) whether the child has a severe discrepancy between achievement and intellectual ability in one or more of seven areas relating to communication skills and mathematical abilities. These concepts are to be interpreted on a case by case basis by the qualified evaluation team members. The team must decide that the discrepancy is not primarily the result of (1) visual, hearing, or motor handicaps; (2) mental retardation; (3) emotional disturbance; or (4) environmental, cultural, or economic disadvantage (Federal Register, 1977, 42, p. 655082).

While this definition provides some guidance, it has generally been regarded as vague, subjective, and as providing for diagnosis by exclusion in many cases. Though these criticisms stem from many areas, they are most loudly exhorted by the LD community itself. Yet, the reason for this definition and its clear emphasis on the establishment of a severe discrepancy between aptitude and achievement can be traced directly to the efforts of the profession in the development of the Federal regulations.

When the rules and regulations for PL 94-142 were being developed, many experts in the field testified before Office of Education hearings, submitted numerous papers and related documentation, and were brought together for discussion and debate at open meetings. When the results of these hearings and debates are examined, the reason for the particular emphasis of the PL 94-142 definition becomes clear. The only consensus regarding definition or characteristics of this thing being called learning disability was that it resulted in a major discrepancy between what would be expected academically of learning disabled children and the level at which they actually achieve.

The importance of the severe discrepancy statement in the above definition was immediately obvious, just as was the potentially subjective nature of the term, especially as it may be applied to individual cases. In an effort to provide guidance in determining a "severe discrepancy" between expected and obtained academic levels, several formulas were proposed and commentary gathered. All of these formulas were ultimately rejected. Some of these formulas defined an expected grade equivalent (EGE); others went on to provide cutoffs for a severe discrepancy. Some of the formulas considered include:

$$EGE = \text{no. of years in school} \times \frac{IQ}{100} + 1.0. \qquad (1)$$

$$EGE = \frac{IQ \times CA}{100} - 5. \qquad (2)$$

$$EGE = (MA + CA + \text{Grade Age})/3 - 5. \qquad (3)$$

$$EGE = (2MA + CA)/3 - 5. \qquad (4)$$

$$\text{Severe Discrepancy} = CA \left(\frac{IQ}{300} + .17 \right) - 2.5. \qquad (5)$$

Formula 5 is the formula for determining a severe discrepancy that was proposed by the Bureau of Education for the Handicapped (now SEP) in 1976 during proposed rule-making for implementation of PL 94-142. This formula was published in the Federal Register and considerable commentary was gathered.

Much of this commentary has been reviewed (Danielson & Bauer, 1978). These various formulas were rejected for a host of interrelated reasons, though most centered around their mathematical inadequacy (cf. Berk, 1984, Chapter 4). These formulas attempted mathematical operations that are not considered appropriate to the level of measurement being employed. The various formulas proffered used age and grade equivalents, which are essentially treated (and inappropriately so) as interval scale and sometimes even ratio scale data (e.g., formula 5).

The various additions, subtractions, divisions, and ratios formed by these formulas are essentially meaningless and in all cases misleading. In the final rules and regulations, no criteria of severe discrepancy were offered and states were left to develop their own, individual criteria for implementing the federal definition. The various states have implemented a number of criteria for diagnosing learning disabilities, each following the federal definition but with great diversity, and adhering to the statutory definition in varying degrees.

The field has thus continued to treat the diagnosis of learning disability from a large number of perspectives and with great subjectivity. The number of children diagnosed and served as learning disabled has more than tripled since 1976 and the likelihood of a child being diagnosed learning disabled now varies by a factor of 5 as a function of the child's state of residence (Reynolds, 1984). Learning disability is rapidly becoming the dominant handicapping condition among the U.S. school-age population, according to data prepared by the USDE, OD/OSE Data Analysis System.

WHY THE LARGE INCREASE IN LD
AND WHY THE TREMENDOUS DISPARITIES
FROM STATE TO STATE?

Prior to the enactment of PL 94-142 and the subsequent issuance of regulations regarding its implementation, learning disabled children were likely underidentified and underserved. Now it appears the pendulum has swung in the opposite direction. The need or desire to provide special education to children having academic difficulties, regardless of the cause of the difficulties, coupled with the loose nature in which the Federal statutory definition has been applied, are almost certainly responsible for the tremendous increase in the number of children classified as learning disabled. Other, societal factors have also entered into this increase to be sure. Most notably, there is a greater resistance now than in previous decades to classification of minority children as mentally retarded. Minority children, relative to white middle and upper-middle class children with similar test profiles, are more likely to be diagnosed learning disabled and referred to a resource room placement (e.g., see Reynolds, 1982, for a review). But again, it is the perceived subjectivity of the PL 94-142 definition (and perhaps lax monitoring and enforcement) that has allowed this to occur.

The implementation of the Federal definition from state-to-state has varied tremendously. Some states have issued statewide guidelines while others leave all decisions to the local districts. Though complete uniformity is not necessarily desirable, adherence to some common diagnostic guides is certainly necessary if learning disabilities as a field of study and a service category is to survive. The statutory requirement of a severe discrepancy between aptitude and achievement is an excellent starting point and one required by the law. Implementation has been difficult and has resulted in the tremendous disparities among the states in the proportion of children served as LD.

The various measurement models in use among the states range from application of the previously rejected Federal formulas to the use of constant grade equivalent discrepancies (e.g., performance two years below grade level for age) to regulations requiring an achievement deficit *and* a processing strength (i.e., a processing skill that exceeds general intellectual functioning) to attempts at application of several different regression models of aptitude-achievement differences. Many variations of the above "models" are evident in state guidelines, though some states provide no guidelines beyond those given in the federal definition. *Each of these procedures, whether intentional or not, sets a mathematical limit on the number of children who can be identified as learning disabled.* Although other factors such as referral rates will affect the actual number of children identified, the range of incidence figures easily can vary from less than 2% to more than 35% of a random sample of the population depending upon which state's criteria are being applied, assuming the use of a single aptitude or intelligence measure and a single achievement measure. As more tests (or multiple scores from but two tests) are employed, these percentages increase dramatically. In the context of a two-hour psycho-educational evaluation, it is not uncommon for the various models to allow an astute diagnostician to qualify between 50 and 80% of a random sample of the population as having a learning disability that requires special education services. Much of this problem is due to a psychometric naivete that permeates much of the rule-making for diagnosis at the State Education Agency (SEA) level. The disparities in psychometric sophistication at the SEA level among states have thus contributed to the radical differences across states in the number of children identified as LD.

As an example of the latter, consider that some states have adopted a model whereby children who exhibit a one standard-deviation (SD) difference between aptitude and achievement (when both tests' scores are expressed on a common scale) are eligible for a diagnosis of LD by a multidisciplinary team. Since one SD below the mean of a normal distribution (assuming we are only interested in cases where achievement is below aptitude) falls at about the 16th percentile, many believe this to create a pool of eligibility of 16% of the population. Other states use 1.5 SDs as a criterion, hoping to generate a pool of about 6% eligibility in the population. (Obviously, setting different cutting scores will create disparities in the numbers of children identified.)

Such inferences are faulty for several reasons. The concept of SD refers to *a* distribution of scores. If two tests' scores are positively correlated, the distribution of scores created by subtracting the scores of a set of students on both tests from one another will not be the same as the two univariate distributions; the SD of this newly created distribution will be significantly smaller than that of the two original distributions. The WISC-R Verbal and Performance IQs (VIQ and PIQ) are normed on the same sample of children and scaled to the same mean (100) and SD (15) and are correlated about .60 to .65. A "one SD" difference between these two scores (15 points) occurs in 25% of the population, independent of the direction of the difference. In a truly random sample of the population (allowing IQ to range from about 45 to 155), the one SD criterion, with the direction of the difference specified, would declare only 12 1/2% of the population eligible. Most criteria however, have an exclusionary clause and do not allow children with IQs in the lower ranges to be considered (e.g., IQ < 85). This will further reduce the number of children eligible, usually quite unbenownst to the individual writing such a rule. Such criteria also fail to consider the regression of IQ on achievement or the joint distributions of multiple difference-score distributions when more than one aptitude or achievement score is being considered. Such factors will also wreak havoc with the anticipated results of the measurement models promulgated under various state guidelines.

The tremendous disparity in measurement models adopted in the various states within their respective LD guidelines and the varying levels of expertise with which the models have been implemented are obvious, major contributing factors to the differences in the relative proportions of children served as LD among the states. Lack of specific definition, improper or lack of application of the severe discrepancy criterion, and the failure to develop appropriate mathematical models (with reference to the severe discrepancy criterion) are the primary, and certainly interrelated, difficulties. More extended discussion of these problems can be found in Reynolds (1984). Given current measurement practices, it seems clear that children with IQs in the 70 to 90 range are presently being overidentified as LD while children with IQs above 100 are systematically denied services. However, in any given state the over- and underserved populations may be reversed, since the specific measurement model in use will dictate the type of systematic error introduced into the diagnostic process (cf., Reynolds, 1984).

OBJECTIFYING DETERMINATION OF A SEVERE DISCREPANCY

Clinical judgement has a revered and an appropriate place in all diagnostic decision-making, even though it has been amply demonstrated that statistical or actuarial approaches are always as good as clinical judgement and often better (Meehl, 1954; Wiggins, 1981). Nevertheless, *people* should hold the central role of decision-making about people. Clinical judgement, however, must be objectified and guided by statistical criteria whenever possible. Given the emphasis of the Federal definition, a uniform approach to determination of a "severe discrepancy" seems a rather opportune point of departure for giving empirical guidance to learning disability diagnosis, particularly when one considers that having a "severe discrepancy" is the only reasonably agreed-upon criterion in the profession.

Most states do, in fact, require a severe discrepancy for a diagnosis of LD. Implementation has always been a problem. To implement such a designation requires considerable statistical sophistication simply not available in the field until now. Computers are so widespread and programs for calculating severe discrepancies so widely available (e.g., Reynolds & Stowe, 1985) that sophisticated, lengthy computational demands on the practitioner need no longer be a problem. It is necessary however to understand how best to calculate a severe discrepancy. It is also worthy to note here and of repeating later, that establishing a severe discrepancy does not diagnose a learning disability; it only establishes that the primary symptom of LD exists. A severe discrepancy is a necessary but insufficient condition for a diagnosis of LD.

To establish that a severe discrepancy exists between two test scores for a particular child, two conditions must be met. First, the simple difference between the two scores must be reliable enough to have great confidence that it is real and not due to errors of measurement; and, second, the difference must be large enough to be unusual among normal or non-LD children.

Formulas such as those noted earlier (i.e., formulas 1–5) and other variations of these formulas that in any way involve the use of grade equivalent or age equivalent scores can be quickly rejected as inadequate and misleading. While the reasons for this are many, age and grade equivalents do not possess the proper mathematical properties to allow their use in any kind of discrepancy analysis, even if they are desirable for other reasons. These problems are discussed at length in a variety of sources and the interested reader will find most relevant information in Angoff (1971), Berk (1984), Reynolds (1981a), and Thorndike and Hagen (1977). In essence, one cannot add, subtract, multiply, or divide age or grade equivalents. In addition to these problems, grade equivalents have other features that make them undesirable, including their ease of misinterpretation, lack of relation to curriculum markers (though appearing directly related), and their more general imprecision. Only standard scores have any real potential for answering the question of severe discrepancy. The following presentations will then deal only in terms of standardized or scaled scores, typically of the age-corrected deviation score genre such as employed by the current Wechsler Scales, the Kaufman-Assessment Battery for Children, and the Stanford-Binet Intelligence Scale (Form L-M), 1972 Norms Edition.

Reliability of the Discrepancy

As noted above the difference between the scores on the aptitude and achievement measures should be large enough to indicate, with a high degree of confidence (i.e., $p < .05$), that the score difference is not due to chance or errors of measurement. This requires an inferential statistical test of the hypothesis that the aptitude and achievement scores for the child in question are the same. This test has been detailed by Payne and Jones (1957) and, though more complex methods of calculation have been proffered involving the reliabilities of the respective scales and the correlation between the two measures (e.g., Salvia & Ysseldyke, 1981), the simpler computational formula below is the algebraic equivalent of the more complex formulas (Reynolds & Willson, 1984; Zimmerman & Williams, 1982). The test for the significance of the difference of

two obtained scores ($X_i - Y_i$), when the scores are expressed as
z-scores is,

$$z = \frac{x_i - y_i}{\sqrt{2 - r_{xx} - r_{yy}}}. \tag{6}$$

In this form, X_i and Y_i represent the child's score on an aptitude
measure X and an achievement measure Y, and r_{xx} and r_{yy} represent
the respective internal consistency reliability estimates for the two
scales. These reliability estimates should be based on the responses
of the standardization sample of each test and be appropriate for the
age of the child being evaluated. Note that reliability estimates based
on item scores across an age range of more than one year will be
spuriously inflated. This and other factors that will spuriously inflate
reliability estimates are presented in several sources (e.g., see
Stanley, 1971, and Willson & Reynolds, in press). These problems
should be meticulously avoided. The test statistic is a z-score that is
referred to the normal curve. For a one-tailed test with $p = .05$, the
critical value of $z = 1.65$. Although a one-tailed test is probably
justifiable when evaluating children referred for the possibility of a
learning disability, one may prefer a more conservative two-tailed
test or a higher level of confidence that the difference is indeed a real
one (e.g., $p = .01$). For a two-tailed test, the critical value of z at
$p = .05$ is 1.96. All other critical values can be determined from any
table of values of the normal curve.

Next, one must evaluate the frequency of occurrence of a
difference score. As this is defined, it will become clear that any
discrepancy meeting the recommended criteria for frequency, will
of necessity also have met the above criterion of reliability.

Frequency of a Discrepancy

In evaluating the frequency of a discrepancy score, one must first
decide just which discrepancy score is to be assessed. For example,
a residualized difference between predicted and obtained achievement scores can be determined, differences between estimated true
scores and residualized true scores, or true difference scores can be
determined in addition to other options. In part, which discrepancy
score is evaluated depends upon the particular interpretation of the
PL 94-142 definition of LD to which one ascribes.

To establish that a discrepancy is severe, one must decide which
of the following questions to address; specifically do we wish to know:

of the following questions to address; specifically do we wish to know:

1. Is there a severe discrepancy between this child's score on the achievement measure and the average achievement score of all other children with the same IQ as this child?
2. Is there a severe discrepancy between this child's measured achievement level and this child's measured level of intellectual functioning?

The mathematical models for answering these two questions differ considerably. The former appears to be the more pressing question when evaluating children with learning problems and is the more consistent with the intent of PL 94-142 (cf. Reynolds, 1984). Evaluating the second question is easier and can be done essentially by following the same methodology as recommended by Kaufman (1979) and others (e.g., Reynolds & Gutkin, 1981) for assessing Verbal-Performance IQ differences on the Wechsler Scales; examples of this procedure can be located in the above sources. As the former question appears more consistent with the intent of PL 94-142, only it will be considered further.

To answer the first question a regression model (i.e., a mathematical model that accounts for the imperfect relationship between IQ and achievement) is required. Once regression effects have been assessed, one can determine the frequency of occurrence of the difference between the academic performance of the child in question and all other children having the same IQ. The correct model specifies that a severe discrepancy between aptitude (x) and achievement (y) exists when, assuming the two tests are scaled to a common metric,

$$\hat{Y} - Y_i \geq SD_y z_a \sqrt{1 - r^2_{xy}} , \qquad (7)$$

where:

Y_i is the child's achievement score,
X_i is the child's aptitude score,
$\hat{Y}$ is the mean achievement score for all children with IQ $= X_i$,
SD_y is the standard deviation of Y,
z_a is the point on the normal curve corresponding to the relative frequency needed to denote "severity," and
r^2_{xy} is the square of the correlation between the aptitude achievement measures.

It is necessary to use $\hat{Y}-Y_i$ as the discrepancy score because IQ and achievement are not perfectly correlated. For IQ and achievement tests each having a mean of 100 and SD of 15 that are correlated .60, the average achievement score of all children with IQs of 80 is 88. For children with IQs of 120, it is 112. Therein lies the need to compare the achievement of the child in question to the achievement level of all other children with the same IQ. The term $SD_y \sqrt{1-r^2xy}$ is the standard deviation of the distribution $\hat{Y}-Y_i$. Since this distribution is normal, we can estimate the frequency of occurrence of any given difference ($\hat{Y}-Y_i$) with great accuracy. Thus z_a can be seen as the number of standard deviations (of $\hat{Y}-Y_i$) that the two scores must be apart to be considered severe. Next, one must establish a value for z_a, a controversial matter in itself.

Establishing a Value for z_a in Discrepancy Models

There are no strictly empirical criteria or research methods for establishing a value for z_a for any of the above models. This is true because we have no consensus of definition of LD generally, and specifically none that would allow the generation of a *true and globally accepted* estimate of the prevalence of the group of disorders subsumed under the term. To complicate this issue further, there is no professional consensus in the LD community regarding whether it is better to risk identifying some children as LD who are not in fact LD (in hopes that nearly all true LD children will receive services) *or* to risk not identifying a significant number of children who are in fact LD (in order to avoid misclassifying as few non-LD as possible). However, under the latter scenario as well as with the assumption of an equal risk model (associated equal risks with both types of diagnostic errors, false positives and false negatives), the proper procedure would be not to identify *any* children as LD since the proportion of the population who exhibit this disorder is so small (see for example Schmidt's 1974, discussion of probability and utility assumptions). Such a professional consensus regarding the desirability of different diagnostic errors, coupled with valid estimates of prevalence would provide considerable guidance in establishing a recommended value for z_a. In the absence of such guidance, one may rely only upon rational, statistical, and traditional criteria for guidance.

It has been previously argued that for a discrepancy to be considered severe, it should occur relatively infrequently in the normal population of individuals under consideration. Of course, *relatively infrequently* is open to the same problems of interpretation as is *severe discrepancy*. Strong tradition and rational argument exist in psychology, particularly in the field of mental retardation, to contend that severity should be defined as two standard deviations from the mean of the distribution under consideration. With regard to a diagnosis of mental retardation, we define a score two standard deviations below the mean of an intelligence scale as a severe intellectual problem making an individual eligible (provided that other criteria are met) for a diagnosis of mental retardation. Qualitative descriptions such as *mentally* or *cognitively deficient* or *lower extreme* are common designations below this point in the distribution. At the opposite end of the curve, most definitions of intellectual giftedness refer to IQs falling two or more standard deviations above the mean, with descriptions such as *very superior* and *upper extreme* being common. There exists widespread acceptance of such practice.

In the field of inferential statistics, confidence levels of .05 in an inference or judgement that an hypothesis is to be rejected are the accepted standard in the field. The .05 number corresponds roughly to two standard errors (for a two-tailed test) of the difference being evaluated or to two standard deviations from the mean of the distribution of the test statistic employed (e.g., z, t, F, etc.). There is, thus, considerable precedent in the social as well as physical sciences for implementation of a two standard deviation discrepancy as a criterion for a discrepancy to be characterized as severe. (For a .05 level of confidence, the actual value of z, 1.96, is certainly close enough to the 2.00 value to support its use.) It is rational then that a value of z_a be implemented to approximate a = .05 and the two standard deviations criterion; thus a value of $z_a = 2.00$ is recommended for determining whether a difference score is severe. This value needs further qualification however.

Since a difference score, whether defined as $\hat{Y} - Y_i$, or some other value, will be less than perfectly reliable, we must somehow consider this unreliability in defining a severe discrepancy. Earlier, a formula for determining the dependability of the difference between achievement and ability test scores was offered (formula 6). As we are now working with Y_i (the actual achievement score of the child) and $\hat{Y}$ (the average achievement score of *other* children of the same ability level), we offer a different correction for error. If we consider it a greater risk to fail to identify as LD a child who is LD than to identify by mistake a child as LD who may not be LD, then we can propose a reasonable correction. Without this assumption, we would minimize total errors by not identifying *any* children as LD. While several methods of accounting for potential unreliability in our discrepancy score are possible, the concept of the confidence interval is both popular and applicable. Adopting the traditional .05 confidence level for a one-tailed test, we can define the value of z_a corrected for unreliability as $z_a - 1.65SE$, which is z_a minus the z corresponding to the one-tailed .05 confidence interval times the standard error of the relevant difference score. (A one-tailed value is clearly appropriate here since we must decide in advance which side to protect; both sides cannot be protected. Under these assumptions, a discrepancy is defined as severe when

$$\hat{Y} - Y_i \geq (2SD_y\sqrt{1 - r_{xy}^2}) - 1.65SE_{\hat{y} - y_i} \qquad (8)$$

The calculation of the standard error of $\hat{Y} - Y_i$ is explained in detail in Reynolds (1984) and need not be repeated. One may obviously choose whether or not to use this correction; however, it does seem reasonable to account for error in the process.

SUMMARY

The procedure outlined above can certainly objectify determination of a severe discrepancy in LD diagnosis. However, it bears repeating here that not all children who have a severe discrepancy between aptitude and achievement are in fact learning disabled. Even a quick reading of the statutory definition shows that many other factors may cause such a discrepancy, and the reasoned use of clinical judgement is clearly appropriate. However, clinical judgement is wrong at least as often and typically more often than empirical, actuarial judgements. We may think we "know one when we see one" but if there is no "severe discrepancy," chances are we are wrong.

Much remains to be considered. Of particular importance is the quality of the data we consider. The mathematical manipulations recommended above cannot transform the quality of the initial data.

Equally important is the quality of the personnel conducting diagnoses. The task of LD diagnosis is the most difficult of all psychoeducational diagnostic tasks and the most highly trained personnel available should be reserved for assignment to evaluating potential LD children. This is clearly not what has been happening in practice (cf. Bennett, 1981; Bennett & Shepherd, 1982).

The state-of-the art in LD diagnosis is also far from perfect and is presently restricted by the tremendous theoretical diversity in the field. However, it seems clear that the state-of-practice in the assessment of LD children lags significantly behind the state-of-the-art for the most part, regardless of one's particular theoretical orientation. The diagnosis of LD in school-aged children is the most difficult to make accurately of all diagnoses provided under PL 94-142. It is alarming to note that this is precisely the area of evaluation and diagnosis most often relegated to the least qualified, least trained, diagnostic personnel in the schools. Arguments as well as data presented by Bennett (1981; Bennett & Shepherd, 1982) clearly show that the learning disabilities specialists and diagnosticians commonly assigned the task of LD diagnosis do not possess the requisite knowledge of tests and measurements to allow them to interpret test scores adequately. On a test of beginning level measurement concepts, Bennett and Shepherd's (1982) LD specialists barely answered 50% of the questions correctly. A group of first year graduate students in an introductory measurement class answered more than 70% of the same questions accurately. Using the best trained staff will not solve the problems involved in diagnosis and evaluation of LD children, but should lessen the gap between the state-of-the-art and day-to-day practice.

The preceding section represents the state-of-the-art in determining a severe discrepancy. Other factors to be considered in this determination will be found in PL 94-142 but will also be dictated by the theoretical approach adopted. It is at this stage inappropriate, to recommend a single, specific theoretical model from which to assess LD. What is evident however is that *a clear theoretical rationale is necessary for coherent diagnosis and evaluation of LD children.* Consequently, at least at the LEA if not the SEA level, the theoretical and conceptual basis for any given criteria for qualification of a child as LD should be clearly stated and understood by district diagnostic personnel and its supporting body of literature cited. It is less important at this stage of inquiry in the discipline just which theoretical or conceptual model is adopted than it is that *a* theoretical model be clearly stated and implemented at a state-of-the-art level. To do less is to cheat the children we seek so hard to serve.

REFERENCES

Angoff, W. H. (1971). Scales, norms, and equivalent scores. In R. L. Thorndike (Ed.), *Educational Measurement* (2nd ed.). Washington, D.C.: American Council on Education.
Bennett, R. E. (1981). Professional competence and the assessment of exceptional children. *Journal of Special Education, 15,* 437–446.
Bennett, R. E., & Shepherd, M. J. (1982). Basic measurement proficiency of learning disability specialists. *Learning Disability Quarterly, 5,* 177–184.
Berk, R. A. (1984). *Screening and diagnosis of children with learning disabilities.* Springfield, IL: Charles C. Thomas.
Chalfant, J. C., & Scheffelin, M. A. (1969). *Central processing dysfunctions in children: A review of research.* (NINDS Monograph No. 9), Bethesda, MD: U. S. Department of Health, Education, and Welfare.
Danielson, L. C., & Bauer, J. W. (1978). A formula-based classification of learning disabled children: An examination of the issues. *Journal of Learning Disabilities, 11,* 163–176.
Kaufman, A. S. (1979). *Intelligent testing with the WISC-R.* New York: Wiley-Interscience.
McLeod, J. (1979). Educational underachievement: Toward a defensible psychometric definition. *Journal of Learning Disabilities, 12,* 42–50.
Meehl, P. E. (1954). *Clinical versus statistical prediction.* Minneapolis: University of Minnesota Press.
Payne, R. W., & Jones, H. G. (1957). Statistics for the investigation of individual cases. *Journal of Clinical Psychology, 13,* 115–121.
Reynolds, C. R. (1981a). The fallacy of "two years below grade level for age" as a diagnostic criterion for reading disorders. *Journal of School Psychology, 19,* 350–358.
Reynolds, C. R. (1981b). Neuropsychological assessment and the habilitation of learning: Considerations in the search for the aptitude × treatment interaction. *School Psychology Review, 10,* 343–349.
Reynolds, C. R. (1982). The problem of bias in psychological assessment. In C. R. Reynolds & T. B. Gutkin (Eds.) *The Handbook of School Psychology,* New York: John Wiley & Sons.
Reynolds, C. R. (1984). Critical measurement issues in learning disabilities. *Journal of Special Education, 18,* 451–476.
Reynolds, C. R. (1985). Measuring the aptitude-achievement discrepancy in learning disability diagnosis. *Remedial and Special Education,* in press.
Reynolds, C. R. (in press). Assessment of exceptional children. In R. T. Brown & C. R. Reynolds (Eds.), *Psychological Perspectives on Childhood Exceptionality,* New York: Wiley-Interscience.
Reynolds, C. R., & Clark, J. H. (1983). Assessment of cognitive abilities. In K. D. Paget & B. Bracken (Eds.), *Psychoeducational Assessment of Preschool Children,* New York: Grune & Stratton.
Reynolds, C. R., & Gutkin, T. B. (1981). Test scatter on the WPPSI: Normative analyses of the standardization sample. *Journal of Learning Disabilities, 14,* 460–464.
Reynolds, C. R., Gutkin, T. B., Elliot, S. N., & Witt, J. C. (1984). *School psychology: Essentials of theory and practice;* New York: John Wiley & Sons.
Reynolds, C. R., & Stowe, M. (1985) *Severe discrepancy analysis.* Philadelphia: TRAIN, Inc.

Reynolds, C. R., & Willson, V. L. (1984, April). *Another look at aptitude-achievement discrepancies in the evaluation of learning disabilities.* Paper presented to the annual meeting of the National Council on Measurement in Education, New Orleans.

Salvia, J., & Ysseldyke, J. (1981). *Assessment in special and remedial education.* 2nd Ed., Boston: Houghton Mifflin.

Schmidt, F. L. (1974). Probability and utility assumptions underlying use of the Strong Vocational Interest Blank. *Journal of Applied Psychology, 4,* 456–464.

Senf, G. (1981). Issues surrounding diagnosis of learning disabilities: child handicap versus the failure of the child-school interaction. In T. Kratochwill (Ed.), *Advances in School Psychology, Vol. 1,* Hillsdale, NJ: Lawrence Erlbaum.

Silverstein, A. B. (1981) Pattern analysis as simultaneous statistical inference. *Journal of Consulting and Clinical Psychology, 50,* 234–240.

Stanley, J. C. (1971). Reliability. In R. L. Thorndike (Ed.), *Educational Measurement* (2nd ed.). Washington, DC: American Council on Education.

Thorndike, R. L., & Hagen, E. (1977). *Measurement and evaluation in education and psychology.* New York: John Wiley & Sons.

Wiggins, J. S. (1981) Clinical and statistical prediction: Where are we and where do we go from here? *Clinical Psychology Review, 1,* 3–18.

Willson, V. L., & Reynolds, C. R. (in press) *Classroom applications of educational measurement.* New York: John Wiley & Sons.

Zimmerman, D. W., & Williams, R. H. (1982). The relative error magnitude in three measures of change. *Psychometrika, 47,* 141–147.

Handicapped Students
and Minimum Competency Testing

Philip J. Grise
Florida State University

ABSTRACT. Minimum competency testing (MCT) programs have become a prominent, if not dominant force in contemporary public education. Provisions made for exceptional students in testing programs by most of the 39 states which have set minimum standards do not afford moderately and severely handicapped students an opportunity to demonstrate competence. The range of accommodation includes some testing programs that categorically exclude the handicapped from participation to others that require their participation with *no* alternations in testing whatsoever. Somewhere in between these extremes lies the provision of braille and large print editions, extra time, testing in brief segments, alternate-format booklets, individual administration, and readers for handicapped students. Another alternative exists as well: defining separate minimum standards for certain segments of the exceptional student population, standards which reflect the different expectations society and educators hold for many special education students and the special curriculum that enables those expectations to be realized.

Testing as a means of identifying and assessing student strengths and weaknesses in academic areas has been a standard procedure for decades. When one hears the word *test*, the standard expectation is to receive a booklet with a security seal on the side, presented with all the aplomb of an execution. In the past fifteen years, the world of assessing the academic competence of students has changed dramatically. This paper discusses some of the issues involved in the minimum competency testing of handicapped individuals.

Requests for reprints should be sent to: Philip J. Grise, Center for Needs Assessment and Planning, Florida State University, Tallahassee, FL 32306.

THE COMPETENCY TESTING MOVEMENT

During the mid-1960's evidence began to appear that elementary school students were not performing as well as their predecessors in the basic skills of reading, writing and mathematics. By 1970, the grumbling had turned into a loud public lament of "Why can't Johnny read?" (Cooperman, 1978). A new term, *accountability*, began to emerge. The public, the underwriters of education in America, wished to obtain assurances that students would have to face measurable criteria and demonstrate that competence existed at least before graduating, if not before promotion to the next grade level (see Brickell, 1978; Fisher, 1978; Marlowe, 1978 for additional perceptions).

States passed legislation mandating assurances of competence for their students; many large city school districts did likewise. By 1984 some thirty-nine states had active legislation regarding competency testing (Pipho & Hadley, 1985). Each state, however, mandated its own methodology for demonstrating competency. Some states set general goals for attainment and insisted that each school district arrive at a means for determining mastery (e.g., Ohio, Nebraska and Massachusetts). This often meant use of off-the-shelf, norm-referenced tests. Other states decided to develop their own testing programs, setting their own performance standards for students. Still other states took a wait-and-see posture. Currently, students in twenty states are required to meet certain minimum competencies before a diploma is issued, or at least will be required to do so by the end of the decade.

Where do the minimum competencies come from? For many years various pools of instructional objectives have existed. These objectives were derived from analyses of standard curricula and logically organized into hierarchies by perceived complexity. Educators have used these objective pools as one valuable resource in setting standards, but have also relied on other information. Subject matter specialists, teachers, testing specialists and school board personnel have gotten together and essentially asked themselves, "What shall we insist upon as minimum capabilities before we issue a diploma?" (Cressey & Padilla, 1981). Some locales have established academic benchmarks at several grade levels before graduation and others have instituted a single exit-examination at some grade before the 12th. Other states or cities have collected minimum competency data but not held individual students accountable.

Instead, descriptions of the senior class' academic performance have been presented, or class-by-class or school-by-school comparisons published in the local media.

Where Do Exceptional Students Fit

With all of the legislative and educational energy spent on developing competency assessment programs, one might think that all possible issues had been addressed. This is unfortunately not the case. Many of the competency programs have accepted the notion that exceptional students should be exempted. Other programs have provided varying degrees of accommodation so that the handicapped person can participate in the minimum competency program. The decision to include or exclude is not always based upon the issue of validity of results, but frequently on availability of resources and willingness to chart unexplored areas (Pipho & Hadley, 1985).

Arguments have been made to delay competency testing programs in their entirety, or at least to exclude exceptional students from some or all of the promotion or graduation requirements until concerns related to the testing of special students can be resolved. These concerns include the potential conflict between the student's Individualized Education Program (IEP) and other state requirements for promotion/graduation; the impact that not passing would have on an exceptional student's future; test validity, adaptability, and special administration issues (McCarthy, 1980); legal issues (McClung & Pullin, 1978); administrative policies (Ross & Weintraub, 1980); and graduation stigma (Smith & Jenkins, 1980).

One of the primary issues discussed in the literature is the feasibility of *multiple* minimum standards. It is often assumed that a minimum competency test measures essential ''life skills'' or ''survival skills'' without which a person cannot be self-sufficient in society. It is also typically believed that a high school diploma signifies the achievement of such skills. Such a contention has never been substantiated (Haney & Madaus, 1978).

Many exceptional students are often not expected to become self-sufficient adults and may live and work successfully in some form of sheltered environment. Special education has never presented itself as a cure for handicapping conditions. Rather, it attempts to provide students with the strategies needed to cope with adult life to the best of their abilities. There are then, a variety of possible standards which can be used to define "self-sufficiency, self-reliance and not under the care, custody or control of others" (Kaufman, 1983). These standards might include academic achievement, personal income, community service, etc.

In keeping with the notion that minimum competency can be defined in different ways, Florida has established certain levels of proficiency for the award of a special diploma. It appears that to date only Florida has created multiple standards (Grise, 1980). Most other states produce large-print and braille editions of their tests, and/or permit additional format and procedural modifications to be made, but do not set different standards for exceptional students (Pipho & Hadley, 1985).

The positive results of Florida's regular education minimum competency program described by Pinkney (1979) have also been experienced in the exceptional student competency program. These results include:

—lists of expected minimum competencies for review by students and teachers;
—a renewed interest in learning on the part of students as evidenced by markedly increased test results;
—greater awareness among parents about student instructional goals and activities;
—more effective utilization of instructional resources; and
—instructionally-useful descriptions of student progress in terms of skill mastery.

METHODS FOR ASSESSING THE COMPETENCIES OF HANDICAPPED LEARNERS

There are several potential ways to approach competency assessment of the handicapped learner (Grise, 1980). The first is to exclude the student from the test. As a last resort, exclusion may be necessary. However, simply excluding the exceptional child from the program without considering alternative methods is a disservice to the student. The entire concept of accountability, like the baby and the bathwater, is discarded by not assessing the competencies of the exceptional learner.

To determine if a handicapped student should be excluded from a testing program, several factors should be considered. First and foremost, a determination should be made about whether the child could be physically or emotionally harmed by the testing experience. Next, the potential usefulness of the data to be obtained from the test should be weighed. Will the test results provide information for initial or remedial instruction? Will decisions of student promotion or retention be based upon the results? Will the student be compared to other students (regular, handicapped-in-general, or handicapped with similar afflictions)? And most importantly, will the test be a valid measure of the competencies that constitute the targets of assessment? Clearly, if the test does not provide useful and valid information, the student should not be tested.

Beyond exclusion, several alternatives exist for including handicapped students in competency testing programs. One alternative is to administer the test to the student in standardized fashion, without making special provisions, such as providing extra time. Another alternative is to administer a special version of the test such as large print, braille, audio or video cassette. With the exception of time limits (consider that reading *braille* generally takes 2–4 times as long), the test administration would remain unchanged.

A final alternative is to use either the standard or modified edition of the test *with* administrative modifications. Such modifications typically include changing or eliminating time limits; administering the test to the student alone or in a small group setting; testing the student in short sessions with extra rest periods; using a revised-format test booklet with fewer items per page, more white space, or items arranged by content area; assisting the student in recording the test answers by transcribing oral responses or transferring from a slate and stylus; providing sample tests for practice prior to the administration; and presenting part or all of the test (depending upon the nature of the skills tested) using either a live reader or an audio or video tape.

SPECIAL DIPLOMAS AND SPECIAL COMPETENCIES FOR EXCEPTIONAL STUDENTS

It can be argued that special education students should be assessed in light of the curriculum presented as part of their course of study. That is, students should only be tested in those areas in which the school system is providing education. Just as the standard diploma serves to motivate students to achieve the minimum competencies for which it stands, the special diploma serves to recognize attainment of appropriate standards for handicapped persons (Westling, 1979). With one type of graduation diploma available, only one set of minimum standards can be used. However, through the use of other graduation/diploma options, special standards can be set.

There has been no public outcry in Florida because of the potential confusion expected to result from multiple minimum standards (McClung & Pullin, 1978). Exceptional students who are capable of meeting Florida's regular "Minimum Student Performance Standards" (Florida Department of Education, 1983), whether through routine or modified testing procedures (e.g., braille edition or extra time), receive the same diploma and are expected to function as successfully as any other student. Severely handicapped students who meet "Special Minimum Student Performance Standards" (i.e., educable or trainable handicapped students and hearing impaired students) may receive a special diploma, which signifies that they have successfully achieved all the state requirements, albeit somewhat below the independent functioning level of standard diploma recipients (Florida Department of Education, 1983; Grise, 1980). These persons cannot necessarily be expected to function in society without support services. Such differences in achievement and functioning have for many years been documented by student transcripts. Two (or more) types of diploma simply reflect the reality that transcripts, the official student records, have always indicated.

School systems must consider past history when planning changes in graduation requirements for students. It is important to consider what documentation was recorded and made available to handicapped students in previous years. Have certain handicapped classifications been given an exit document other than a diploma? For example, have trainable mentally handicapped (TMH) persons received a certificate of attendance rather than a high school diploma? Does the school transcript display the courses taken and grades obtained by students? Are transcript course titles descriptive enough to allow an employer to discriminate between TMH high school math (which might consist of very basic number facts) and general math?

If the school district has not provided high school diplomas for handicapped students, then very possibly no future graduation document would be required beyond the satisfactory completion of the student's IEP. If, however, all students exiting grade 12 have received a high school diploma, the school district may be obligated to provide special mechanisms by which new candidates can receive a graduation document. These mechanisms take the form of a special diploma or a modified transcript. In such cases, graduation requirements must be developed to emphasize desirable goals for the handicapped person.

Setting Special Standards for the Handicapped Learner

Two main avenues exist for setting special standards. One method involves a procedure sometimes referred to as *off-level testing*. A standardized test, norm or criterion-referenced, is administered to a student whose age or grade is higher than that for which the test was originally designed. For example, a sixth grade hearing-impaired student might be presented with a second-grade edition of a reading test. In off-level testing it is important to consider the utility of the data that are generated. Are the data provided useful for competency purposes if a sixth grade deaf student takes a second-grade test?

Should the resulting data be deemed useful, then off-level testing could be a simple means of accommodating the testing problems of handicapped students. However, many times the particular weaknesses of the exceptional student are not merely an overall reduction in academic level. Conceptual understanding might be age-appropriate but specific vocabulary, or mastery of other academic domains might be deficient. These developmental subtleties might not be detected by the lower-level test.

The problem becomes all the more exaggerated when an educable mentally handicapped high school student is faced with that same second grade test. Not only does the 17 to 19-year-old face content targeted to the interest of an 8-year-old, but the test is likely to measure basic reading, writing and mathematics skills. Most retarded high school students are involved in work-study programs and primarily receive instruction in social/personal and prevocational skills. The second grade test would probably be at the correct readability level, but would not address these skills. "Instructional validity" would be nearly impossible to demonstrate since the test would not be evaluating areas in which the student is receiving significant instruction (Popham, 1981).

Just as educators have agreed on minimum standards (usually in language arts and mathematics) for regular students, so too can they agree on defining minimum standards for handicapped individuals, standards that *do* have instructional validity. If the basic premise of competency testing is to evaluate whether the student has retained the education provided by the school district, then minimum competencies should be set that relate directly to the specialized programs exceptional students receive. Although these minimum standards would be below those established for regular students, there is little danger of destroying the meaning of the regular standard. So long as we consider the program in which the student is operating, the courses the student takes, and the long-range goals available to the student—including the type(s) of diploma available—there should be no confusion between the two sets of standards.

How are these special minimum standards set? The Florida Department of Education is the only large educational body that has developed special standards for exceptional students to date. Three separate sets of special minimum performance standards were created in the late 1970s. Standards for hearing-impaired, educable mentally handicapped, and trainable mentally handicapped students at several grade levels each, have been produced. Each set of standards was developed in much the same way as standards for regular students. Selected teachers, curriculum specialists and testing experts met togther on several occasions to review various curricula from many school districts. Drafts of recommended global objectives and specific skill statements were prepared to represent the essential minimum skills. These drafts were widely circulated throughout the entire consumer group (the appropriate special educators for each handicapping condition). Revisions were made and the standards circulated once again. The final products have been in use for nearly a decade.

Through the methods employed in Florida, minimum competency standards for handicapped students can be set. These standards can be used to allow handicapped students to participate in minimum competency testing programs and thereby demonstrate the extent to which they have mastered the goals of special instruction. Finally, such standards permit handicapped students—like regular students—to strive for and receive recognition for their achievements.

REFERENCES

Beattie, S. (1982). *The effect of physical test format modifications on the performance of third grade mildly handicapped and normal students.* Unpublished doctoral dissertation, University of Florida, Gainesville, FL.

Brickell, H.M. (1978). "Seven key notes on minimum competency testing" *Phi Delta Kappan, 59,* 589–591.

Cooperman, P. (1978). *The literacy hoax: The decline of reading, writing and learning in the public schools and what we can do about it.* New York: Morrow.

Cressey, J., & Padilla, D. (1981). *Minimal competency testing and special education students: A technical assistance guide.* Menlo Park, CA: SRI International.

Fisher, T.H. (1978). Florida's approach to competency testing. *Phi Delta Kappan, 59,* 599–601.

Florida Department of Education (1983). *Minimum student performance standards.* Tallahassee, FL: Author.

Grise, P.J. (1980). Florida's minimum competency testing program for handicapped students. *Exceptional Children, 47*(3), 186–191.

Grise, P.J., Beattie, S., & Algozzine, B. (1982). Assessment of minimum competency in fifth grade learning disabled students: Test modifications do make a difference. *Journal of Educational Research, 76,* 35–40.

Haney, W., & Madaus, G. (1978). Making sense of the competency testing movement. *Harvard Educational Review, 48,* 462–484.

Kaufman, R. (1983). *Planning for organizational success.* New York: Wiley & Sons.

Marlowe, J. (1978). Back to basics. *Phi Delta Kappan, 59,* 627.

McCarthy, M.M. (1980). Minimum competency testing and handicapped students. *Exceptional Children, 47,* 166–173.

McClung, M., & Pullin, D. (1978, March 6). Competency testing and handicapped students. *Clearinghouse Review,* 922–927.

Pinkney, H.B. (1979). The minimum competency movement in education. *Clearing House, 52,* 413–416.

Pipho, C., & Hadley, C. (1985). State activity: Minimum Competency Testing. *Clearinghouse Notes.* Denver, CO: Education Commission of the States.

Popham, W.J. (1981). The case for minimum competency testing. *Phi Delta Kappa, 76,* 35–40.

Ross, J.W., & Weintraub, F.J. (1980). Policy approaches regarding the impact of graduation requirements on handicapped students. *Exceptional Children, 46*(3), 200–203.

Smith, L.D., & Jenkins, D.S. (1980). Minimum competency testing and handicapped students. *Exceptional Children, 46,* 440–443.

Westling, D. (1978). *Problems and issues related to minimum performance testing and exceptional students in the State of Florida.* A special report to the Florida Task Force on Educational Assessment Programs, Tallahassee, FL: Department of Education.

Standards for Educational
and Psychological Testing:
More Than a Symbolic Exercise

Roland K. Yoshida

Fordham University

Douglas L. Friedman

Fordham University

ABSTRACT. The 1985 edition of the American Psychological Association's *Standards for Educational and Psychological Testing* has greatly expanded its coverage of the testing of special populations including handicapped students. The enforcement of the *Standards* depends upon professionals themselves. Yet, recent surveys of practitioners' knowledge of basic testing and measurement concepts raise serious questions about the extent to which they are prepared to administer and interpret not only standard versions of tests but also modified ones. Extensive in-service training to upgrade skills is recommended.

Documents such as the 1985 edition of the *Standards for Educational and Psychological Testing* (American Psychological Association, 1985) are essentially symbols. They do not list acceptable tests, nor condone particular ways of testing such as using a computer. Rather, they represent the profession's general consensus of good practice at a certain time and come with very little enforcement authority. As with any professional code, the *Standards* depends upon its users to insure that tests are appropriately employed. "The *Standards* should . . . embody a strong ethical imperative, though it was understood that the *Standards* itself would not contain enforcement mechanisms" (1985, p. 1 of the Preface). If readers approach the *Standards* with this perspective, they will not be frustrated when

---

Requests for reprints should be sent to: Roland K. Yoshida, School of Education-Lincoln Center, Fordham University, 113 W. 60th St., New York, NY 10023.

187

they want a definitive answer as to whether a certain practice meets a given standard.

Nevertheless, the *Standards* does provide readers with important reference points for evaluating whether new testing philosophies and methodologies such as those presented in this volume meet minimal levels of acceptable practice. The *Standards* also raises issues that the profession perceives as requiring further inquiry and discussion. As test users analyze the 1985 edition of the *Standards*, they will come to appreciate the complexity involved in making the testing process fair and equitable for those with handicaps.

Besides general standards relating to validity, reliability, and test administration, the 1985 edition appears to have restated some standards, and expanded and added others which directly address testing the handicapped. Table 1 presents five categories of standards and the corresponding citations from the 1974 and 1985 editions.

Of the five categories, only one, the advisement that no single measure be used to evaluate a person, has remained the same in the 1974 and 1985 editions. It is not surprising that this standard was retained. The original impetus for including such a standard was probably the series of federal court decisions dealing with the overrepresentation of minority group students, especially black and Hispanic, in classes for the mildly mentally retarded (Meyers,

Table 1

Citations for Five Test Categories of Standards
in the 1974 and 1985 Editions

Issue	1974 Edition	1985 Edition
1. No Single Measure Used to Evaluate Individual	H2	8.12
2. Methods for Classifying Handicapped Individuals	D2; D2.2.1; E1.2	1.3; 7.2; 7.3; 7.4; 8.3; 14.6
3. Test Modifications for the Handicapped	E2.3	6.2; 14.3; 14.4
4. Test Data Used to Develop Education Programs		8.11
5. Notification of Testing and Test Results		7.5; 8.6

Sundstrom, & Yoshida, 1974). Plaintiffs in the *Larry P. v. Riles* (1972) case argued that placement was made based upon only the measured I.Q. of the student. Although the American Association of Mental Deficiency definition of mental retardation at that time (which was later incorporated into P.L. 94-142) refers to subaverage intellectual functioning *and* impairment in adaptive behavior (Heber, 1961), very few mildly mentally retarded students were assessed on the latter dimension. Research on adaptive behavior measures has generally shown that results from these measures do not correlate highly with intelligence tests (Kicklighter, Bailey, & Richmond, 1980; Oakland, 1980). When measures of adaptive behavior are included as part of the assessment process, large proportions of mentally retarded students, especially non-native speakers of English, no longer meet criteria for the category (Childs, 1982; Coulter, 1980; Fisher, 1977; Scott, 1979a, 1979b). Finally, most classification systems, such as that presented in the *Diagnostic and Statistical Manual of Mental Disorders* (American Psychiatric Association, 1980), recommend the use of multiple criteria.

Besides the category discussed above, two categories have been expanded to include direct references to the handicapped or statements published in law or the professional literature concerning the handicapped. The first of these categories focuses on the methods by which handicapped persons are classified. For example, in the new edition, Standard 8.3 points out the validity and reliability problems inherent in interpreting aptitude-achievement differences. This standard is a direct reference to the federal definition (Federal Register, 1977) of learning disability (LD). In addition, both Standards E1.2 (American Psychological Association, 1974) and 1.3 (American Psychological Association, 1985) state that test users must adequately justify their interpretations " . . . of subscores, score differences, or profiles. . . . " (p. 1–8). The comment accompanying Standard 1.3 contains a caveat about the validity of the severe discrepancy criterion contained in the definition of LD: "Such differences should be found substantially more often in known learning disabled test takers than in other test takers before such differences can be taken as indicative of a learning disability" (p. 1–8). Singling out the LD definition for such comment may show the profession's grave concern over the ambiguous results of using various discrepancy formulas (Berk, 1981; Cone & Wilson, 1981; Forness, Sinclair, & Guthrie, 1983; Reynolds, 1981;

Shepard, 1980; Wilson & Cone, 1984; Ysseldyke, Algozzine, & Epps, 1983) and WISC-R profiles (Anderson, Kaufman, & Kaufman, 1976; Gutkin, 1979; Miller, 1980; Smith, 1978; Tabachnick, 1979; Vance, Wallbrown, & Blaha, 1978) in identifying LD students.

Similarly, the 1985 edition devotes more attention to test modifications for the handicapped. In the 1974 edition, Standard E.3 prescribed, "When a test user plans to make a substantial change in test format, instructions, language, or content, he should revalidate the use of the tests for the changed conditions" (p. 33). In the new edition, Standard 6.2 basically reiterates Standard E.3. If taken literally, these standards pose a dilemma. It is essential to have tests with psychometrically sound properties. However, if one were to multiply the number of tests that are routinely administered to handicapped persons by the number of handicapping categories and the number of possible modifications, the resulting figure would represent the number of times revalidation would have to occur. Efforts to investigate modifications are just beginning (Allen, White & Karchmer, 1983; Bennett, Rock, & Kaplan, in press; Bragman, 1982; Grise, Beattie & Algozzine, 1982; McKinney, 1983; Mishra, 1983) and represent less than 1% of all possible combinations given the above algorithm.

It appears that the committee recognized this enormous problem to some extent when it added Standards 14.3 and 14.4. Basically, the two standards combined are intended to guide test developers and users in the steps minimally required for evaluating a procedural modification and reporting results when reliable psychometric data are impossible to obtain because of small samples. Small samples are likely to occur when testing those with low-incidence handicaps such as sensory or physical disorders. The accompanying comment to Standard 14.3 states, "Even when such [pilot] tryouts [of modifications] are conducted on samples inadequate to produce norm or validity data, they should be conducted to check the mechanics of the modifications" (p. 14-4). Finally, the comment to Standard 14.4 states, "If empirical evidence of the nature and effects of changes resulting from modifying standard tests is lacking, it is impossible to enumerate significant modifications that are to be documented in manuals. Therefore, test developers should take care to document all changes made and be alert to indications of possible effects of those modifications" (p. 14-4).

The remaining two categories of standards apparently were added in response to practices resulting from P.L. 94-142. In terms of the relationship between assessment and the development of individualized instructional programs, Standard 8.11 cautions test users not to base the selection of instructional objectives and strategies on test results which have not been validated for that purpose. Standards 7.5 and 8.6 follow the prior notice and informed consent regulations of P.L. 94-142. They direct test users to promptly report to clients, namely students, parents, and teachers, not only test results but also descriptions of what tests were used, what they are intended to measure, and how scores are to be interpreted.

In short, these five categories of standard serve to reinforce several legal regulations as well as professional consensus concerning testing practice. However, similar to the federal approach to enforcing P.L. 94-142 (see any edition of the U.S. Department of Education's *Annual Report to Congress*, U.S. Department of Education, 1979–84), the task of complying with these *Standards* is left to competent test users and their supervisors (see Standards 3.25, 6.6, 6.10, 8.1, 8.2, 14.1, 14.7). Within this context, Bennett and his associates (Bennett, 1981, 1983; Bennett & Shepherd, 1982) research and commentary raise serious questions about the qualifications of school personnel to administer and interpret test results. For example, Bennett and Shepherd (1982) compared the performance of LD Specialists on a test of basic measurement concepts (e.g., validity, reliability, norms, measures of central tendency) to that of graduate students in an introductory measurement course. On the average, the LD Specialists answered about half of the items correctly and scored significantly lower than the graduate students. In addition to this finding, Bennett (1981, 1983) has summarized research relating to other test-user inadequacies, such as selecting inappropriate instruments when technically sound ones were available, and misinterpreting test results. Even a skill such as correctly scoring a test protocol seems to create problems for some test users. If such basic skills are lacking in test users, can we be confident that they will be able to appropriately administer modified some tests, interpret results beyond those purposes recommended in test manuals (such as using WISC-R profiles for LD placement), or judge when they are not qualified to do so? Will test users appropriately use innovative procedures such as those discussed in this issue of *Special Services in the Schools*?

Given the lack of sanctions in the *Standards*, the onus is upon training institutions to monitor the progress of their candidates in developing not only basic measurement proficiencies but also new skills demanded by the *Standards* and the profession. For those professionals who have a license or credential, additional training in methods of testing the handicapped may be needed. Otherwise, the *Standards* will remain a symbol, a creed not realized in practice.

REFERENCES

Allen, T.E., White, C.S., & Karchmer, M.A. (1983). Issues in the development of a special edition for hearing-impaired students of the seventh edition of the Stanford Achievement Test. *American Annals of the Deaf, 128*, 34–39.

American Psychiatric Association. (1980). *Diagnostic and statistical manual of mental disorders*, (3rd ed.). Washington, D.C.: Author.

American Psychological Association. (1974). *Standards for educational and psychological tests*. Washington, D.C.: Author.

American Psychological Association. (1985). *Standards for educational and psychological testing*. Washington, D.C.: American Psychological Association.

Anderson, M., Kaufman, A.S., & Kaufman, N.L. (1976). Use of the WISC-R with a learning disabled population: Some diagnostic implications. *Psychology in the Schools, 13*, 381–386.

Bennett, R.E. (1981). Professional competence and the assessment of exceptional children. *Journal of Special Education, 15*, 437–446.

Bennett, R.E. (1983). Research and evaluation priorities for special education assessment. *Exceptional Children, 50*, 110–117.

Bennett, R.E., Rock, D.A., & Kaplan, B.A. (In press). *The psychometric characteristics of the SAT for nine handicapped groups*. Princeton, NJ: Educational Testing Service.

Bennett, R.E., & Shepherd, M.J. (1982). Basic measurement proficiency of learning disability specialists. *Learning Disability Quarterly, 5*, 177–184.

Berk, R.A. (1981). What's wrong with using grade-equivalent scores to identify LD children? *Academic Therapy, 17*, 133–140.

Bragman, R. (1982). Review of research on test instructions for deaf children. *American Annals of the Deaf, 127*, 337–346.

Childs, R.E. (1982). A study of the adaptive behavior of retarded children and the resultant effects of its use in the diagnosis of mental retardation. *Education and Training of the Mentally Retarded, 17*, 109–113.

Cone, T.E., & Wilson, L.R. (1981). Quantifying a severe discrepancy: A critical analysis. *Learning Disabilities Quarterly, 4*, 359–371.

Coulter, W.A. (1980). Adaptive behavior and professional disfavor: Controversies and trends for school psychologists. *School Psychology Review, 9*, 69–74.

Federal Register. (1977). *42*(250), 65082–65085.

Fisher, A.T. (1977). *Adaptive behavior in non-biased assessment: Effects on special education*. Paper presented to the annual convention of the American Psychological Association. (ERIC Document Reproduction Service No. ED 150514).

Forness, S.R., Sinclair, E., & Guthrie, D. (1983). Learning disability discrepancy formulas: Their use in actual practice. *Learning Disabilities Quarterly, 6*, 107–114.

Grise, P., Beattie, S., & Algozzine, B. (1982). Assessment of minimum competency in fifth grade learning disabled students: Test modifications make a difference. *Journal of Educational Research, 76*, 35–40.

Gutkin, T.B. (1979). WISC-R scatter indices: Useful information for differential diagnosis? *Journal of School Psychology, 17*, 368–371.

Heber, R.F. (1961). A manual on terminology and classification in mental retardation. (rev. ed.). *American Journal of Mental Deficiency Monograph* (Supplement 64).

Kicklighter, R.H., Bailey, B.S., & Richmond, B.O. (1980). A direct measure of adaptive behavior. *School Psychology Review, 9*, 168–173.

Larry P. V. Riles, U.S.L.W. 2033 (U.S. June 21, 1972).

McKinney, J.D. (1983). Performance of handicapped students on the North Carolina minimum competency test. *Exceptional Children, 49*, 547–550.

Meyers, C.E., Sundstrom, P.E., & Yoshida, R.K. (1974). The school psychologist and assessment in special education: A report of an Ad Hoc Committee of Division 16. *School Psychology Monographs, 2*(1), 3–57.

Miller, M. (1980). On the attempt to find WISC-R profiles for learning and reading disabilities (A response to Vance, Wallbrown, and Blaha). *Journal of Learning Disabilities, 13*, 52–54.

Mishra, S. (1983). Intelligence test scores as a function of variation in test administration procedure. *Journal of Clinical Psychology, 39*, 603–607.

Oakland, T. (1980). Evaluation of the ABIC, pluralistic norms, and estimated learning potential. *Journal of School Psychology, 18*, 3–11.

Reynolds, C.R. (1981). The fallacy of "Two years below grade level for age" as a diagnostic criterion for reading disorders. *Journal of School Psychology, 19*, 350–358.

Scott, L.S. (1979a). *Adaptive behavior assessment and the implementation of P.L. 94-142.* Paper presented at the annual meeting of the Texas Psychological Association. (ERIC Document Reproduction Service No. ED 185738).

Scott, L.S. (1979b). Identification of declassified students: Characteristics and needs of the population. Paper presented at the annual meeting of the American Psychological Association. (ERIC Document Reproduction Service No. ED 185737).

Shepard, L. (1980). An evaluation of the regression discrepancy method for identifying children with learning disabilities. *Journal of Special Education, 14*, 79–91.

Smith, M.D. (1978). Stability of WISC-R subtest profiles for learning disabled children. *Psychology in the Schools, 15*, 4–7.

Tabachnick, B.G. (1979). Test scatter on the WISC-R. *Journal of Learning Disabilities, 12*, 60–62.

U.S. Department of Education. (1979–1984). *Annual report to Congress on the implementation of Public Law 94-142: The Education for All Handicapped Children Act.* Washington, D.C.: Author.

Vance, H.B., Wallbrown, F.H., & Blaha, J. (1978). Determining WISC-R profiles for reading disabled children. *Journal of Learning Disabilities, 11*, 55–59.

Wilson, L.R., & Cone, T. (1984). The regression equation method of determining academic discrepancy. *Journal of School Psychology, 22*, 95–110.

Ysseldyke, J., Algozzine, B., & Epps, S. (1983). A logical and empirical analysis of current practices in classifying students as handicapped. *Exceptional Children, 50*, 160–166.